Solution Selling…
Data Networks and Services

By Dean W. Evans

Solution Selling...Data Networks and Services.

Copyright © 2012 by Dean W. Evans

All rights reserved. No part of this book shall be reproduced, stored in a retrieval system, or transmitted by any means, electronic, photocopying, recording, or otherwise, without written permission from the publisher. No patent liability is assumed with respect to the use of the information contained herein. Although every precaution has been taken in the preparation of this book, the publisher and author assume no responsibility for errors or omissions. Nor is any liability assumed for damages resulting from the use of the information contained herein.

ISBN: 978-1-291-17981-1

First Edition

Trademarks

All terms mentioned in this book that are known trademarks or service marks have been appropriately capitalized. The publisher cannot attest to the accuracy of this information. Use of a term in this book should not be regarded as affecting the validity of any trademark or service

Warning and Disclaimer

Every effort has been made to make this book as complete and as accurate as possible, but no warranty or fitness is implied. The information is provided on an 'as is' basis. The author and the publisher shall have neither liability nor responsibility to any person or entity with respect to any loss or damages arising from the information contained in this book.

Contact Information

Should you wish to contact the author, you may do so via their website http://www.deanwevans.com/ or via email to info@deanwevans.com

Table of Contents

About The Author 5

A Living Book 7

Introduction 9

Solution Selling – a quick introduction 13

Part 1 – The Data Network Marketplace 17
    TELECOMMUNICATIONS COMPANIES 17
    HARDWARE COMPANIES 20
    INTERNET SERVICE PROVIDERS 23
    SOFTWARE COMPANIES 26
    SYSTEMS INTEGRATORS 29

Part 2 – Technical Solutions 33
    NETWORK BASICS 33
    POINT TO POINT SERVICES 40
    ETHERNET SERVICES 45
    IP VPNS 49
    INTERNET CONNECTIVITY 54
    DATA CENTRES AND HOSTING 59
    CLOUD SERVICES 63
    VIRTUALISATION 67
    UNIFIED COMMUNICATIONS 71

Part 3 – Selling 77
    BASIC SELLING SKILLS 77
    SOLUTION SELLING 82
    RESEARCH 85

MAKING CONNECTIONS 88
'C' LEVEL SELLING 90
   Selling to the CEO *90*
   Selling to the CFO *93*
   Selling to the CIO/CTO *96*
SELLING TO THE IT DEPARTMENT 101
SALES HINTS AND TIPS 103
FURTHER READING 106

About The Author

Dean W. Evans has been involved in the IT industry for over 20 years. Initially starting out in IT support for the Board of Directors of a multinational corporate, he then moved into technical sales, initially in consultancy before moving into direct sales and managing sales teams. Working for numerous blue chip companies such as British Telecommunications PLC, Barclays PLC and Vodafone Group, Dean has worked on IT and Telecoms sales all the way up to multiple million pound solutions. He still works in the industry, along with being a trainer and coach and speaking at sales events across the world.

With two grown up children, Nick and Chris, both heavily into IT, they keep him on his toes from a technical viewpoint. Dean additionally hosts a podcast on the technology industry and its impact on people in their home and working life, along with running a number of websites dedicated to sales and technology.

A Living Book

Please note, this is a 'living book'. What I mean by this is that what you are getting when you buy this is not just a dormant book, but one that is supplemented by online material, updated over time where necessary and discussed by its community.

To become part of this, simply visit the website;

http://www.deanwevans.com/

and register yourself as part of the community.

You will then receive updates to this book in your email inbox, as and when they are needed, along with further information about this subject. You will also get the chance to ask questions of the author and other members of the community, to help you in your sales career and understanding of this fascinating area.

Introduction

Data networks are one of the core elements of most companies. Regardless of what they do and in what industry sector they are, the need for companies to communicate, both inside their own organisation and outside, is at the heart of the modern business. From simply being able to send emails to colleagues and clients, through interacting with other offices and systems and up to machines talking to each other to make things happen (M2M communication), a reliable data network is essential.

Data networks have been key since the 1970s and were initially the domain of the telecommunications companies (these Telcos are still an intrinsic part of this service although there are now other types of organisations involved in this arena through the increase in the types of technologies available to build these networks) as they used the connectivity (the copper and fibre lines which the Telcos had installed in the ground or along telegraphy poles) built for the telephone systems as the delivery mechanism for data networks.

Before we go any further, let's narrow down what we mean by data networks in this context. The modern data network is one where people, via devices, can communicate with other people or computers and systems via a spider's web of cables, satellites, cell towers and Wi-Fi hotspots. But that definition maybe too big to comprehend. Let's look at a data network in its most simplistic form. Let's imagine you have a computer and your colleague across the room has a computer. If you connect these two computers together with a cable, you have a basic data network. A network, because one device can talk to another, and a data network as the way they communicate is by sending each other data, usually in the form of ones and zeros (or binary) as this is the language that electronic devices understand. Data networks are therefore inherently DIGITAL, in that they use discrete ones and zeros, as opposed to the telephone network as it originally was, which was ANALOGUE as it used electricity to deliver a sound 'wave' from one point to the other.

Because these data networks were initially built on the telephone networks of the past, people who are used to selling voice services (person to person communication) are now being asked to sell data services (person to machine or machine to machine communication). These are inherently very different products and require a different knowledge base as well as different sales techniques to successfully sell them.

This book is therefore aimed at people who find themselves, either through career choice or through career movement, selling data networks. To complicate matters further, most voice services now use a data network as the infrastructure to deliver them. However, to successfully sell data networks, one does not have to become a network guru (there are many out there and, quite often, you will get access to one to support you in your sales when needed). What you need to know in regards to data networks to be able to sell them is really broken down into the following;

- The basic idea how a specific type of network works.

- What benefits your customer will get from it.

- How one type of network is different to another.

- What the customer is getting when they buy from you.

- How to articulate all of this in a way your customer cares about.

This last is by far the most important. Unless you are selling to clients who specialize in data networks (maybe Internet Service Providers, Resellers or Systems Integrators), your customer doesn't actually CARE, nor do they want to care about the technology underneath it all. What they care about is what it will do for them and their business, what problem it will solve or what enhancement it will bring to them as a company. That doesn't mean you shouldn't know and understand the product you are selling, but it means that the depth of your understanding does not need to be that of a 'guru' in the field (although to be a 'guru' on a subject, all you really need to know about that subject is 1% more than the person you are talking to).

This book is therefore not designed to make you an expert on data networks. If that were your goal, then I would firstly question if you should be in the sales environment in the first place. There are thousands of books and courses which will go into the intricacies of Dense Wave Division Multiplexing, Multi Protocol Label Switching and all the other network types you can come across. What this book IS designed to do is give you;

- An understanding of the aspects of data networking AND HOW THEY BENEFIT YOUR CUSTOMER.

- To be able to understand the different types of network and where one may be better in a situation than another.

- The key things that a data network service provides and how to express those to a non-technical customer (i.e. 99.999999% of customers).

- Enough information to 'hold your own' when faced with a technical customer

- How to 'solution sell' data networks

- The various 'services', the things you can do with a data network (or sell with a data network) that provide a benefit.

- The sales messages YOU NEED to successfully sell data networks and their associated services.

To make all this happen, the book is broken into three sections. The first section is about the companies involved in data networks and their associated services worldwide. The reason for this is to give you a solid background and foundation of the industry you are involved in. The second section looks at the various data networks and associated services you are likely to come across, including Internet connectivity,

Data Centres and Ethernet Services. We will also look at the big 'buzz words' in the industry and what they mean, such as 'Cloud', 'Virtualisation' and 'Unified Communications'.

The third and most important section concentrates on how to sell the services we have been looking at. We will first look at some basic sales skills that everyone need to become a successful solution seller, before moving on to specifics in regards to selling these solutions at various customer levels, be it CEOs, Directors, Department Heads or the dreaded 'IT Department'. We will finish with some hints and tips you can use in your sales meetings and calls TOMORROW to increase your success rate.

You are also encouraged to ask questions of me and others in the industry via the blog at www.deanwevans.com, where you can sign up for regular newsletters, tip sheets and participate in forums and discussions on technical sales in general.

So, whether you're an established sales person looking to give your skills and knowledge a brush up, or a new to the role salesperson looking to increase both your skills and therefore your earnings, good luck to you all and let's get started!

Solution Selling – a quick introduction

We will talk many times in this book about 'solution selling'. We will look at the solution selling techniques for various products and services in each section but before we go on, what is solution selling?

To explain, let's look at buying a car. When you look into buying a car, you may look at various facts and figures, such as how many seats it has, the engine size, the warranty period and so on. When you look at these, you are creating an objective tick list in your mind as to what your new car needs to have before you are going to buy it. These aspects of this 'product', because a car is just a product, are all important and anything you sell must also 'tick the boxes' in regards to the product category you're selling. But why did you go into a showroom in the first place?

You probably went in because you needed a car to get you to work in the morning and home again at night. You needed one that allowed you to go to visit relatives or go out to have fun on the weekend. Maybe because you want to drive across the continent on holiday, or just to do your weekly shopping. But you could do all these things on public transport, on a bicycle, or by walking. The reason that you went in really is to get FREEDOM. Freedom to go where you want to go, when you want to go, and not have to rely on anyone else. You want to be able to go out on your own or with your family and just drive. That's the solution the car offers, freedom from being tied to public transport or to a geographic region.

The problem is, selling a solution is a lot harder than selling a product. Now sometimes, selling products is fine, especially in the car market. If car A can get to 60mph in .5 of a second faster than car B, then you can make a sale on that basis. But you're still really selling a solution as, in this case, what you're selling is the bragging rights that one driver wants to have over another in having the faster car. But if you said that to someone, that they should buy car A because they can boast more about it to their colleagues, not everyone will like that thought (although some will of course, we all know 'those' people!).

Keith M. Eades, author of The New Solution Selling, defines a solution as:

"So what is the definition of the word solution? The typical response is, "An answer to a problem." I agree with this response but feel it's important to expand the definition. Not only does the problem need to be acknowledged by the buyer, but both the buyer and working woman must also agree on the answer. So a solution is a mutually agreed-upon answer to a recognized problem. In addition, a solution must also provide some measurable improvement. By measurable improvement, I mean there is a before and might be after. Now we have a more complete definition of a solution; It's a mutually shared answer to a recognized problem, and the answer provides measurable improvement."

Although somewhat long winded, I tend to agree with this. One mistake not to make though is to think of the word 'problem' in just the negative way. Although we may be addressing a problem a lot of the time, we will also be addressing a positive problem for the customer, such as 'how to increase our sales' or 'how to give our staff more freedom'. You could of course reword these into negatives ('our staff don't have enough freedom of where they work') but making sales on a positive footing will usually be a move advantageous approach to selling your particular solutions.

So solution selling is the method of moving away from specifics of a product and concentrating instead on what 'problems' a potential customer needs to have solved to the benefit of their company. One of the primary reasons this is advantageous in the data networking and associated services arena is that, quite often, the products we are selling are extremely complex and difficult to understand. If you try and sell them by talking about these aspects, you first have to educate the customer into why an RJ45 connected router is better than one with BNC connectors on it...and what RJ45 and BNC connectors actually are!

The problem facing salespeople is that they need to both understand the solutions, AND understand the technology (to a degree at least), as they are the conduits to translate the product into the solution for the customer. But that isn't easy. Some sales people struggle with the products and the technical aspects and then find it hard to translate to solutions. And others find the technology really simple, but then sell based on the technology and not understand the solution.

Throughout this book, we will try and combine the both, looking at the product and what it does, but then looking at the solutions associated with that product and the problems they address. By having a comfortable understanding of this duality, a salesperson can be both players in the process, the bringer of technology and the solver of problems. That is the challenge in front of the IT salesperson.

Part 1 – The Data Network Marketplace

Telecommunications Companies

Data Networks and their associated services are traditionally the purview of the telecommunications companies. British Telecommunications Ltd in the UK, AT&T and others in the US and other Telcos (short for Telecommunications Companies) around the world. Often initially government owned companies, these organisations had the remit to provide communications services across a country, digging paths to lay cables or erecting poles to carry cables, the huge cost outlay to build the infrastructure was a massive undertaking. As such, many countries only had one monopoly or often a duopoly of companies with the backing to build these networks of cables.

Over time, technology evolved to allow these vast spider webs of cables to carry more than just voice across the country and, eventually, the world. However, the Telcos whole business model was based around a switched network, that is, a network where the devices on the end of the service, the telephone handsets, were only in use some of the time and had the ability to connect to any other end point through connections being 'switched'. Data networks however are based around a continuous, single point to single point communication. But nevertheless, the development of computers and electronics meant that, regardless of the fact that the network wasn't built to do it, the telecoms companies saw the massive need that was approaching and that they, with their nationwide web of cable, were perfectly placed to take advantage of the business opportunity.

However, this wasn't without its problems and still, in the beginning years of the 21st century, traditional telecommunications companies are still adjusting their networks to suit the need for data as opposed to voice.

Telcos hold the position in the market of owning the physical cables in the ground. This means that many other businesses, such as Internet Service Providers, Systems Integrators and others, rely on the telecoms companies to provide the infrastructure to deliver their services. But the Telcos themselves are also providers of the same services that these companies provide, which create a continual state of unease between the telecoms companies and the 'wholesale' users of their services. This unease has continually spilt over into legal and regulatory issues that, at the time of writing in 2012, show no signs of abating.

The primary issues facing Telcos are that of scale and reach. In many countries, the major Telcos have a regulatory responsibility to have to provide service to all inhabitants of the country, regardless of location. Although there are different ways to do this, the cost of providing access to someone in the far-flung corners of a country can be extremely prohibitive. Nevertheless, regulation compels them to do it. This has created a multi-level Telco offering, with tier 1 companies wholly owning the network they use and the associated regulations it needs to adhere to, and tier 2 Telcos owning some network infrastructure they themselves have installed in the ground and also procuring services from the tier 1 companies, taking advantage of their reach and existing infrastructure and often having less regulation in place around the services they offer.

In this market place, we will also come across terms like OLOs (Other Licensed Operators) and MOLOs (Mobile Other Licensed Operators). These terms cover the various telecommunications companies that build networks and have a license to offer services in a country, but often take their core infrastructure from the tier 1 companies.

Finally, you may come across companies called VNOs, Virtual Network Operators. These are companies whom solely use another company's infrastructure to provide a service, but then rebrand it to them to take advantage of their position in the wider market place. A good example of this is the supermarket chain Tesco who, in the UK, offer a mobile phone services. However, they are actually a VNO and are just rebranding the services of the mobile operator O2, owned by the Spanish Telco, Telefonica.

Hardware Companies

Although the telecommunications companies have had the jump as far as the network cables are concerned, the hardware that connects to the end of these cables to send and control the data has not been their strong point. This market has been dominated by a number of companies, most noticeably Cisco, Huawei, Ericsson and Juniper. These companies were much better placed to build and deploy the equipment that enabled computers to talk to each other due to the slow adoption of these services by the Telcos.

Cisco in particular is the biggest player in the hardware market. Based out of San Francisco and established in 1984, Cisco has been the leader in developing the technologies that enable computer networks to work. One of the strongest points they have is that they have always been agnostic of the network providers given that the telecoms companies were building their networks around agreed standards (separate in the US to Europe and the Far East, but similar enough so as to not cause a problem), meaning that they could sell world wide and, more importantly, the engineers who worked and configure these devices could learn them once yet work on them anywhere. Even today, Cisco accreditation is still one of the most lucrative qualifications in the network world for a person to achieve and accredited engineers are constantly in demand.

However, like any company that becomes big and dominant, their ability to react quickly to changes and the need for them to standardize their product set has allowed other companies to come into the market. Huawei is the biggest hardware supplier in the world when you take into account both data networks and voice network equipment (Cisco is very much a data network company). Founded in 1987 in China, the company is now based in the UK, primarily because its relationship to the Chinese government has caused it some problems in acquiring business, especially in the government networks of other countries, where trust and secrecy regarding the data network infrastructure is of a high concern.

The network hardware provided by these companies usually falls into the following general categories;

Gateways: a device (read 'box') sitting in a network that translates from one type of network to another

Router: the key part of many networks, a router is the sorting office of the network world, looking at the data that is coming through and sending it out the cable it needs to go to get to its intended destination

Hub: a 'one to many' device that allows multiple other devices to connect to it and talk directly to each other. Unlike a switch, it's a somewhat 'dumb' device in that it doesn't control the traffic in any way and is more just an aggregator of connections

Switch: similar to a hub but it also contains a level of intelligence to control the traffic

Bridge: a device that connects network 'segments' (parts of networks) together to build bigger networks.

Repeater: a device that 'boosts' the signal in a network, ensuring it has the 'energy' to get to its end destination.

There are of course many other devices within the portfolios of these companies that do wonderful things, like provide video conferencing service, Voice over IP (VOIP) services, and many others. However, for the purpose of our sales knowledge, the product groups above are all we really need to know.

We will look more at other specific devices when we look at particular solutions later in this book.

As data services providers, Telcos, ISPs and systems integrators are all major customers of the hardware suppliers. However, many companies prefer to own their own hardware to give them access to configure it how they wish and, as such, the hardware providers sell directly to the end customers as well. This creates both problems and opportunities in the data network space. Problems because some solutions companies offer will require them to 'lock down' the end hardware so the customer cannot access it (especially in cases where they are charging the user based on the speed of service). Opportunities come with the massive buying power of the network companies, which makes them an excellent route to market for the hardware companies and, as such, have preferential rates on buying equipment that can be passed on to the end client.

Internet Service Providers

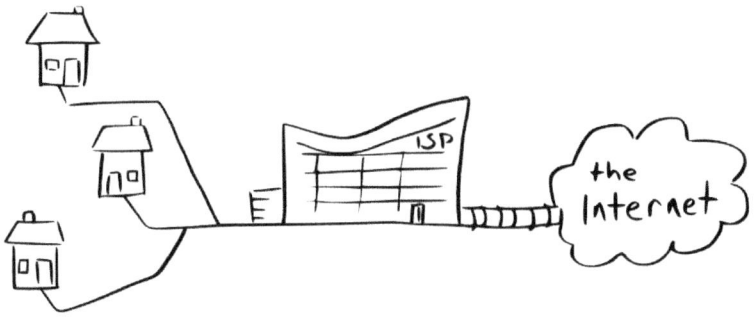

The biggest network that most people are aware of is the Internet (see the chapter on 'Internet Connectivity' for a more detailed understanding of what the internet actually is). Because of its popularity and the fact that 'the public' wanted access to it, companies were formed that specialized in proving access to this worldwide resource. What they primarily did was two fold. Firstly, they provided a way for a 'user' (be it an individual in their home, or a company and their whole office) to send traffic from their computer and get it to its destination, wherever in the world that was. In addition, ISPs provided other services on top that the average user wanted, such as email accounts or website hosting.

Although we will go into more detail later, the Internet is really a 'network of networks'. What this means is that an ISP (such as AOL) connects all of its users to each other. An ISP in the UK (such as Easynet) connects all of its users together. What these companies also do is create a connection between them so that, if an AOL customer wants to communicate with an Easynet customer, they can. These connections (interconnects or peering agreements to give them their correct term) were originally informal agreements between companies. AOL may connect to 10 other companies as well and, if Easynet connects to them, they not only get a communication path to AOLs customers, but also to the customers of those 10 other companies. This system is how the Internet we know today was born, a network of networks where companies agree to interconnect with each other so their customers can communicate.

The interconnection of these networks is now big business, with companies charging each other depending on how much traffic is going between them and in what direction (as in, if company A is sending more traffic to company B than the other way, company B may charge company A a fee as A's customers obviously want access to B's customers more than the other way around).

Since the advent of broadband services (high speed connection over old copper telephone lines), the amount of traffic traversing these networks has grown exponentially. Also, the variety of things you can do on the Internet, from video and voice calls, to viewing movies, accessing your bank or doing your shopping (ecommerce), has made Internet connectivity and controlling it to make the best use of it, extremely big business. However, the commoditization of the actual network (the connection to your home or office) has meant the margins possible for companies is extremely small and more and more are having to rely on 'value adds', the extra things they can get you to purchase on top of your internet connection, to make their profit.

Value adds, such as email accounts, anti-virus solutions, spam filtering, firewalls (hardware or software that protects your network from unwanted visitors) and web hosting are all ways ISPs try and differentiate from each other to create a 'sticky' user experience. We use the term sticky in this context as churn amongst end customers, particularly in the consumer space, is rife and as much as possible, ISPs create services that the customer is unwilling to lose if they leave or are such that the pain of changing from one ISP to another (like having to change email address) is more effort than the user is willing to go though and as such, will 'stick' with what they have.

When looking at the practicalities of being an ISP, they are big users of the services of Telcos and hardware companies. The first point of connection for a customer is the box in their home or office. This box is provided by one of the hardware suppliers mentioned previously (or one of the other, smaller providers in this space). The ISP buys this from the hardware company, which is then configured by the ISP as to how the service should run for their customer, and then shipped to the user to be plugged in. What it is plugged into is a cable provided by one of the Telcos. The other end of the cable is the office of the ISP, where they aggregate all the various cables from their customers and plug them together into one big network.

Of course, in this market place, Telcos themselves also provide Internet connectivity. This could lead to dominance from the Telcos but, fortunately, regulation of the market ensures that they must wholesale their services at such a rate as to allow other companies to compete in this arena.

Software Companies

Software companies and data networks are intrinsically linked. Data networks are the enabler for software to break out of the confines of the physical equipment it is on and communicate with others to get things done. We can break the software provided down into two distinct areas, that of the operating systems that make the equipment run, and the applications that run on top of the operating system that the user interacts with to achieve a specific result. Having said this, the move to 'cloud' has blurred this by adding in a layer in between, the browser. But more on this later.

Although there are multiple operating systems in the world, it is dominated by three variants, Microsoft and its Windows system, Apple and its OSX platform and Linux (there are others, especially in the world of servers, but these three dominate). So as to be clear, the operating system is the interface between the user and the computer its self. Without it, you would need to know how the ones and zeros of electrical pulses traverse the circuits of the computer hardware and store themselves on the memory of the system. Operating systems are therefore in place to make 'operating' the computer as easy as possible. Although most people are aware of the user versions of these three giants, there are also versions of these three specifically designed to act as servers, that is, computers that 'serve' information to multiple others.

Once a computer has an operating system, it then needs to have applications. These are the software programs that sit on top of the operating system and actually 'do' things that the user wants, be it producing documents, drawing pictures or adding up tables of numbers. Applications designed to work with one of the three operating systems cannot work on the others. Some manufacturers will produce versions of their applications to work on others (such as Microsoft, who make a version of it popular Office package to run on the Apple platform), although in general, software producers specialize in one type of operating system.

One of the most used 'applications' on a modern computer is the web browser. The web browser (Internet Explorer, Safari, Firefox, Opera, Chrome, to name but a few) is an application just like any other on a computer (the same as Word or Excel). However, this applications specific task is to look at information that is out on the Internet and show it to the user in a way for them to easily understand. The 'cloud' movement (which we will talk more about later) has meant that the browser has taken more and more of a prime spot in the users mind as, far from just showing webpages to the end user, as was originally intended, it has grown to allow interaction between systems far away across the internet and a user, via these web browsers.

Regardless of if via a web browser or directly from within another application, the ability for your local software to talk to software on other computers is key. It also means that there are considerations in the data networking world to take in regards to these operating systems and applications and their requirements.

The wild west of the software environment in the early 2010s is in the mobile space. Apple with its IOS system on iPhones and iPads, Google with its Android operating system and Microsoft with its Windows 8 platform are all vying to become the choice for mobile software. As in the computer space, the operating systems have applications loaded on top of them and an application written for one of these eco systems will not work on the other two.

Despite this fragmentation, when it comes to the more complex solutions that data networks enable, such as Unified Communications and Video Calling to name just two, the solution provided must be able to work across any device, on any platform. Put simply, if you were today to make a software application such as Skype (a application to allow you to voice call people via your computer and talk to them using your computers microphone and speakers), you would need to build at least 6 different variants of the application, one each for Windows, OSX and Linux, and one each for iPhone, Windows Phone and Android. A complex solution indeed!

Although complex, this fragmentation has been the key to the speed at which software has developed over the years. Competition in this space is fierce and has driven constant change. A market without this competition would be stagnant, something that no one wants, not even the software companies themselves, as constant innovation has lead to constant income opportunities.

Systems Integrators

Systems Integrators have come into the market over the past decade or so to try and cope with the complexity of the IT market in general. They tend to follow two types of business model, either as a consultancy, advising and project managing solutions for a customer, or in a reseller basis, where they not only advise and project manage, but also hold the commercial contract with the suppliers and onward bill this to their clients.

In some ways, all of the companies we have spoken about so far, be them Telcos, ISPs, hardware or software companies, all have designs on being Systems Integrators, wanting to take end to end ownership of a companies whole IT solution, both from the point of view of wallet share (the amount of money they can bill their client as a percentage of what the client has to spend), but also from a control and delivery point of view. This is rarely going to happen though as each supplier has different strengths and weaknesses and this approach does not make for a good risk profile for a company as they are wholly reliant on one supplier and are effectively 'at their mercy' should there be any issues with the stability of the company.

One successful organisation that has made the transition from a hardware supplier to a systems integrator is IBM. International Business Machines (IBM) started life making and distributing counting machines in 1911. However, very soon after their inception, IBM combined with other companies (such as a The International Time Recording Company) to being to offer business solutions as opposed to pure products and services. Today, IBM is one of the most successful technology consultant companies, in addition to still manufacturing its own equipment and still producing its own software for specific uses (although they have moved out of the desktop computer business).

The real difference between systems integrators and consultants is the ownership level in regards to the end solution. A consultancy would tend to help design and build a solution for a client but will not take ownership of the solution. Systems Integrators will tend to also take ownership of the end solution and the on going running of the service and its maintenance.

From a client's point of view, systems integrators can be both a curse and a blessing. The need for a holistic view of the market is great and the complexity of it is such that using an SI to bring it all together, choosing the best offerings from all the potential suppliers and finding the 'best of breed' solution, along with integrating all of the new solution in with the existing infrastructure and services, is an extremely compelling idea. However, this also comes at a cost as the systems integrator has to include a margin in the solution as a whole to make them a profitable organisation as well. It is a fine line for a customer to tread, but the knowledge that a systems integrator can bring to the table cannot be underestimated and has a value that could be said to be above that of which they charge. Although I am painting a positive picture of the SI community here, there are also many negative players in this market, simply taking the solutions of others and offering them as their own with little value added. Even worse, the neutrality of the SI is often in question with agreements and deals from their suppliers being a part of the market as a whole, clouding the judgment of these solutions.

Because of their position, SIs are major customers of all the other companies we have so far discussed, Telcos, hardware companies, software companies and Internet Service Providers. The interaction between all these companies makes for a diverse and interesting marketplace, with more possible combinations of services and suppliers than it is possible to count. And furthermore, it also creates a wealth of opportunity for the successful sales person in this arena to work their magic!

Part 2 – Technical Solutions

Disclaimer: This book is not here to make you a technical expert, just to give you an understanding of how and where different data networks and services would be used and the principles behind them. The following chapters rely heavily on analogies and simplification when it comes to the explanation of services.

Network Basics

Before we get into the intricacies of specific network types, let's look at some basic things we need to know. Networks are ways of connecting together individual computers and systems, floors of an office, whole buildings, buildings to each other and even sites across the world. Although over the years there have been various terms and buzzwords, we can really break networks down into two types, the LAN and the WAN.

The LAN stands for Local Area Network. This effectively means computers and other devices that are located locally to each other. The term 'local' can be very broad. A LAN can encompass just one small office, or be as big as a whole campus complex with 10 or more buildings. It really means that it spreads across an area that is owned by one organization.

However, if the organisation owns more than one office, site or campus and they are geographically spaced apart from each other, you need a WAN or Wide Area Network to get them to communicate with each other. A WAN can encompass two sites in the same town, or be as large as two offices on different continents, it doesn't matter. To be a WAN, they simply need to be geographically remote from each other.

Although the various points on a WAN could be an individual computer, more often than not, WANs connect LANs to each other. So, a company has an office in London and another in New York. Within the London office, there is a LAN enabling information to spread between the computers and systems of that building. The New York office also has a LAN for the computers there to talk to each other. A WAN link is then put in place so that the London computers can communicate with the New York computers.

Network Designs

Things become a little more complex when you have more than two sites. Although networks in companies tend to grow organically and change over time, there are a few principles when it comes to building effective networks.

Point-to-Point Network Design

We will talk about point to point connections more in the next chapter but simply put, this is where each site has a connection to each other site. Although this means that data always has a route to get to its destination the problem is that, as you add a new site to a network, you have to add multiple new connections to that site so it can talk to each other site on the network.

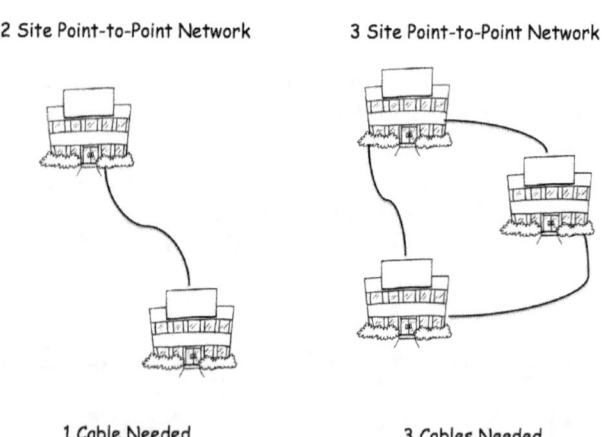

2 Site Point-to-Point Network   3 Site Point-to-Point Network

1 Cable Needed   3 Cables Needed

Hub and Spoke Design

A more efficient way to build a network is with the 'hub and spoke' method. In this case, one site (the 'hub') acts as a central point for the others. Each 'spoke' site has a connection to the hub site and, if traffic needs to get from one spoke site to another spoke site, it travels through the hub. This is much more efficient but not without its own problems. Should there be a problem at the hub site, everyone's ability to talk to each other is effected.

Hub and Spoke Point-to-Point Network

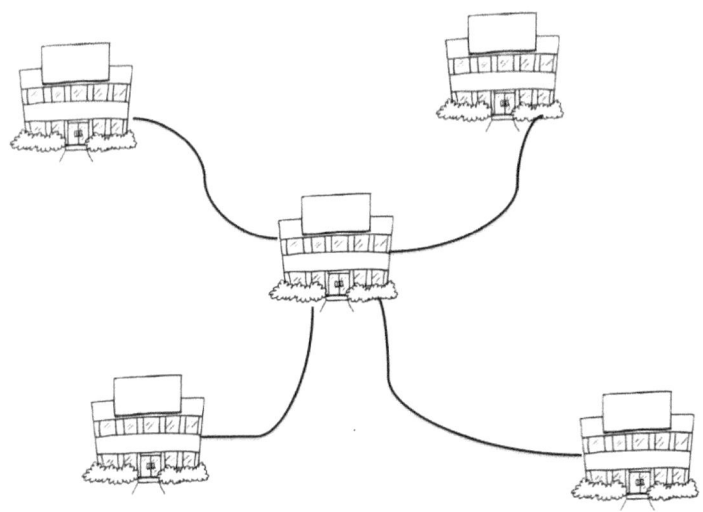

Most network managers tend to build an element of 'resilience' into their network designs to get around this problem. One common way is to have more than one hub site and each spoke connects to more than one hub. In this case, if one hub goes down, the traffic can flow via the other hub instead. Although overall a good solution, this can also be expensive as, in this case, you may have links in the chain which you are paying for but are dormant most of the time and not being used to full capacity.

A good network design is therefore a compromise between resilience and cost effectiveness. Solutions include having multiple connections from a site, but one being 'primary' and the other being 'secondary' and the secondary being a slower, less expensive type of connection that is just used in an emergency. Should there be a problem and they need to use the second link, work will slow down but at least things are still live for the user and they are able to work, even if at a slower speed.

Ways to connect

Once we have decided the design of our network, as in, what site will talk to what site and the level of resilience we need, we then need to look at how we are going to connect the sites together. This falls into two categories, each with their own sub types. We can either have a physical connection (an actual cable), or a wireless one (using one of the available wireless technologies).

Wired connections.

Wired connections come in primarily two flavours (or a combination of), copper and fibre. Copper is the traditional method of connection. For a copper cable to send information, an electrical pulse is sent along the cable from a transmitter, and is received at the other end by a receiver, which interprets the signal. However, this method has some inherent flaws. Firstly, the electrical signal degrades over distance so you have a limit as to how far it can go without needing some sort of 'boost'. Secondly, there is a limit to how fast the signal can go, governed by the laws of physics. And finally, copper is prone to degrade over time, thus needing repair and replacement. However, copper is by far the most widespread technology available due to the fact it has been around for so long, is comparatively cheap to produce and install and is abundantly available. (Note: there is a side issue in that copper is of course a valuable metal and it is not unheard of in some countries for it to be regularly stolen, melted down and sold on the black market).

A more efficient connection is made by using fibre optics. Fibre optic cable works by the transmission of a pulse of light as opposed to electricity. This is much faster than electricity, has a much longer working distance and the cable itself is more resilient, being made of glass or plastic. Fibre came into the market in a cost effective way in the late 1970s and early 80s and was a step change in the speeds available for networks. However, the change from copper to fibre has been slow due to the sheer volume of copper already installed. Many companies worldwide install fibre as a standard in all their services, whereas most traditional Telcos will use the cheapest possible method, which could be copper, depending on the required speed. At this moment in time, copper is still a cheaper delivery method for services, although the gap is swiftly closing.

Wireless Connections

Wireless connections take advantage of the various wave spectrums available. Currently, connectivity tends to break down into 4 wireless types; satellite, microwave, Wi-Fi and cellular.

Satellite communications were the big step forward when it came to global communication. Before satellite, signals that need to travel around the world used cables that were laid under the sea by massive trawlers, spooling cable from the back of them. The biggest negative was that, if there was a problem with the cable, getting to it was an extremely expensive and difficult task. Since the advent of satellites, global communications took a huge step forward until, today, there are well over a thousand communications satellites orbiting the earth. Still primarily used for large communications links, two-way satellite communications is now coming into the public arena, with satellite phones becoming cheaper and a wider availability of satellite based Internet connectivity.

Microwave connectivity is a point-to-point service for use in situations where the two sites are 'in straight line sight' of each other. A transmitting and receiving dish is placed on the top of each site and aimed towards each other. Once aligned, microwave signals are used to transmit data between the two sites. Extremely cost effective, microwave is especially useful in areas where placing telegraph poles or digging into the earth is difficult, such as city centres. However, there is an issue with finding a 'line of sight' between locations and also in regards to interference from atmospheric conditions.

Wi-Fi has become the darling of network builders for being very cheap and easy to deploy, especially in the LAN environment, where distance isn't so much of an issue. An 'access point' makes a connection, via a wireless adaptor, to each device in its local area. Once that connection has been securely made, the device and the access point can send data between them as they would on a wired network. Currently Wi-Fi technology is primarily used in the local area (effective range is usually little more than 20-30 meters). However, there are Wi-Fi standards available which allow communication over vast distances (the current record for two Wi-Fi devices is 304km). The investment in the infrastructure and the development of network technology from the mobile carriers has made this a less attractive option and has kept traditional Wi-Fi as a LAN based technology.

Cellular communication and its standards (GSM, CDMA, 2G, 3G, HSPA, LTE, 4G, etc.) are designed around the fact that the devices that use them are not constantly in the same place. An area is split into 'cells' (hence the term, cellular technology) and each cell has a base station. As you exit the range of one cell and enter the range of another, the cell base stations communicate with each other and seamlessly hand over the responsibility for communication between them. Until recently, because of this need to be able to cope with devices on the move, the speeds available have been comparatively low. But with the growth of 4G (4th Generation) and LTE (Long Term Evolution) networks, speeds for cellular services are now in the multiple megabit range and therefore make them a viable replacement for other communication methods.

Network Types

Finally in this chapter, let's look at the two core types of network, public and private. Private networks are the traditional domain of most companies. The IT department of a company that owns a private network has total control over that network and all data that runs over it. They control which devices connect to it, what types of data it will transmit, from which sites to which sites communication can happen and how well it all works together.

The biggest public network everyone is aware of is the Internet. We will look at how the Internet works in later chapters but it is fundamentally a public solution in that anyone (at a cost) can get access to it. This makes it inherently unsecure and not useable for companies whom need to keep their information secure.

Having said this, these two networks are becoming more and more entwined. Firstly, most office people also need access to the public Internet to find out information and communicate with people outside their organization. Also, with the workforce of the 21st century becoming more mobile, workers may not always be in an office location when they need to access their companies' data. To facilitate this, various technologies have been developed to allow people to use the public internet, but in a secure way, by encrypting their information or by the private networks allowing some information to enter from the internet, providing it is 'approved' by the internal IT department.

Point to Point Services

The simplest (from a technical viewpoint) way to build a network is to connect a cable all the way from one office to another. This is known as a point to point service as all data flows from one point to another (both ways). These simple network connections are the fundamental services offered by suppliers and often the basis for more complex solutions as well. We will look at wireless services later but a point-to-point connection can also be achieved using wireless technology. However, virtually all point-to-point services are delivered by copper or fibre optic cables. But, if a customer has a point-to-point connection going from, say London to Edinburgh, do they actually get a single cable travelling all that way (about 400 miles)? Well, in one way, yes they do. However, where possible, the supplying company will take advantage of more complex technologies to allow parts of this big long cable to be shared by multiple customers and thus achieve an economy of scale (and so you don't need to dig up the road every time a new connection is made). If you want to learn more about this, you can look up the term 'multiplexing'. However, this is not something you need to concern yourself with in selling point to point services. As far as your customer is concerned, they are actually getting a cable running 400miles between these two sites.

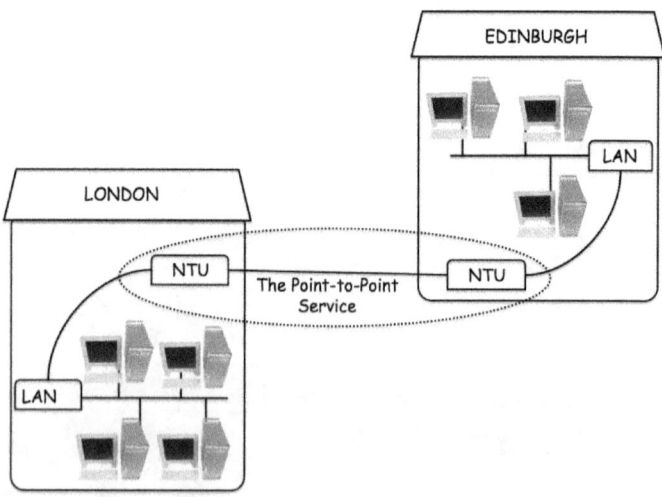

So distance is obviously a cost factor when it comes to these services. The second is speed or, more correctly, bandwidth. What we need to understand when it comes to speed is that we are actually talking about how much data can be pushed down the connection in an one second. Speed is measured in kbps (kilobits per second), mbps (megabits per second) and gbps (gigabits per second), each of these being 1000x faster than the one before (so 1000kbps = 1 mpbs). The actual cable does not care what speed of data is sent down it, it is the box at each end that decides how fast it can understand the data presented to it.

The box at each end is often called an NTU (Network Terminating Unit) but can have many other names, such as CPE (Customer Premises Equipment), NTE (Network Terminating Equipment) and many others. But, for our needs, it is simply the box that is on each end of the cable, the actual device the customer sees in their office. If we buy a 2mps service from a supplier, they make sure there is a cable (copper or fibre) going from one office to the other, and then put a box on each end of it, into which the customer plugs in their own equipment (usually their LAN). If a customer then wants to upgrade the speed from 2mbs to, say 8mps, all you need to do is change the box at each end. This is a simplistic point of view as the supplier will need to check that all along the cable (at the various junction points along the way) it can handle the higher speeds, but again, from a sales point of view, that is what is happening.

Although the NTUs have changed and become more complex over time, the laws of physics create certain barriers when it comes to how fast we can push data through a cable. For most suppliers, if the speed is under 2mbps, then it is cheaper and more effective to use a cable made of copper to deliver the service. If however, the customer requires a higher speed, it is more effective to use a fibre optic cable. This is why there can be a big jump in prices between some speeds, because it's not just as simple as changing the boxes, a whole new cable may need to be provided. Copper uses pulses of electricity to send the signal, where as fibre optic uses pulses of light, and light can travel faster than electricity!

Across the world, these point-to-point connections run on slightly different standards, hence you will hear different terminology used, especially between UK and US companies. So, for example:

In the UK, the standard point-to-point connection of around 2mbps is called an E1 circuit. In the US, it's called a T1.

34 mbps, in the UK it's a E3, in the US it's a T3
155 mbps, in the UK it's an STM1, in the US it's an OC3

Don't let these terms fool you. They are often used interchangeably and no one can ever remember them all!

HOT SALES TIP: Buy a copy of 'Newton's Telecoms Dictionary'. Released yearly, Newton's records all the various acronyms and naming conventions in one big dictionary. As a data salesman of many years, I always have a copy sitting on my desk.

Pros of Point-to-Point Services. *You get what you pay for.* As these lines are dedicated for each clients use, if you pay for 2mbps, you can get 2mps flowing through it 24 hours a day, 7 days a week.

They have higher guarantees. As they are dedicated and also the 'simplest' of the network connections, the suppliers can usually offer higher levels of guarantees on the service. The guarantees are usually around 'up time' (what percentage of the time each year they will guarantee it will be working) and throughput (the speed you will get between the two ends of the service). Up time is measure in percentages and, for point-to-point services, 99.999% (five 9's) is about as good as it gets.

Top-level security. With point-to-point services, your data is segregated from that of others through the physical cable. Short of actually connecting rogue equipment into the cable (and knowing exactly where and how to interpret it), point-to-point connections are the most secure network type you can run.

Cons of Point-to-Point Services. *Paying Too Much.* If you don't need to use all the available bandwidth, all the time, you will often be paying for more than you need. The supplying company doesn't care if you use it or not, you still have to pay for it.

More Sites, More Circuits. In a small network of just a couple of sites, point-to-point is fine. However, problems arise if you want to add a new site to your network. Although you need one cable to connect two sites, if you want them to also talk to a new third site, you need two new cables, one to each of the existing sites. This becomes exceptionally complex and expensive the more sites that come on board, unless you look at traffic traversing over other sites (so traffic goes from site 'a' to site 'b' and then onto site 'c').

Extra Equipment Needed. These traditional point-to-point services were designed around voice-based services. As such, they need extra equipment added to them to enable them to work in the data environment. As an example, if you want to connect two LAN's together, you need to add an extra box between the NTU and the LAN to be able to 'translate' the signal from the service to one the LAN will understand.

Key Sales Words and Messages

- Secure
- Dedicated
- Resilient
- Tried and Tested

Constant connectivity between sites with equal bandwidth 24/7/365.

Provides traditional voice services as well as data.

Uses any existing investment in traditional equipment.

Solution Sales Messages

Your customer has a only few specific sites that would benefit from direct communication.

They mention security as a major factor for them or are specifically in the financial field or work closely with government organisations and thus need to adhere to security criteria.

They talk about being let down by other suppliers and are keen on guarantees around the services they purchase.

Ethernet Services

As highlighted thought out this book, the primary use of data networks is to connect together LANs at geographically disburse sites. Given this, many suppliers produce services that are specifically designed for this purpose. But before we go any further, let's take a quick look at the term 'Ethernet' and what it means.

When networks were originally being built, there were many different standards being defined. Each standard had its own pro's and con's associated with it but, like VHS vs. Betamax, one standard usually wins out. In this case, the standard was Ethernet. Ethernet is the connection that 99.99% of equipment uses to 'talk' to the network. It's the cable that comes out of your computer and plugs into the socket in the desk along which data flows. Typically a copper cable consisting of eight thin cables wrapped in a soft, pliable outer casing with a plastic connector at each end (termed an RJ45 connector). Ethernet is built into virtually all equipment, as it is a comparatively simple and cheap connection mechanism for computers and other devices.

Given this, it would be much easier if the 'box' that a supplier of a WAN service provides a customer is also of the same type, namely Ethernet. It's easier if the IT department of a company only has to be concerned with one type of network when it comes to understanding and supporting it. So WAN Ethernet services were developed.

They tend to come in two flavours, point to point Ethernet Services and Network Cloud based Ethernet services. However, from the customer point of view, the key thing is that the LANs at each end of the connection can talk to each other as though they are just on one big LAN together. In fact, when set up, a computer on one LAN has no idea if the computer it's talking to is on the next desk or in the next city.

Point to point Ethernet services are the simplest to understand. Like the traditional point-to-point services of the previous chapter, a physical cable connects sites together. The main difference is that the 'box' on the end of the circuit 'understands' the Ethernet language and the customer has no need to put an extra box on the end of the service to do any translation. However, that approach suffers from the same issues when it comes to building out to multiple sites, as in, you need multiple connections from each site to the other. It also has a problem that the speed of a LAN is usually a minimum of 10mbps and therefore needs to be built exclusively around fibre optic cables as opposed to copper cables, even though copper cables are by far more available in the ground as the older, more established, technology.

Network Cloud based Ethernet services get around some of these problems by providing one physical connection (cable) that is broken down into virtual 'sub' cables in the box at the customer's premises. If that sounds too complex, think of it like this. If you want to connect to two other sites from your own site, instead of having one socket on the box provided to plug into, you have two sockets, one which goes to site x and one to site y. Actually, they all go along the same cable and meet in the middle in a big 'network cloud' (think of this as a mythical place where all cables connect to each other in a big cable spider web). Once in the cloud, the network is intelligent enough to know where the data has come from and where it needs to go and sends the data accordingly, like an electronic postal sorting office.

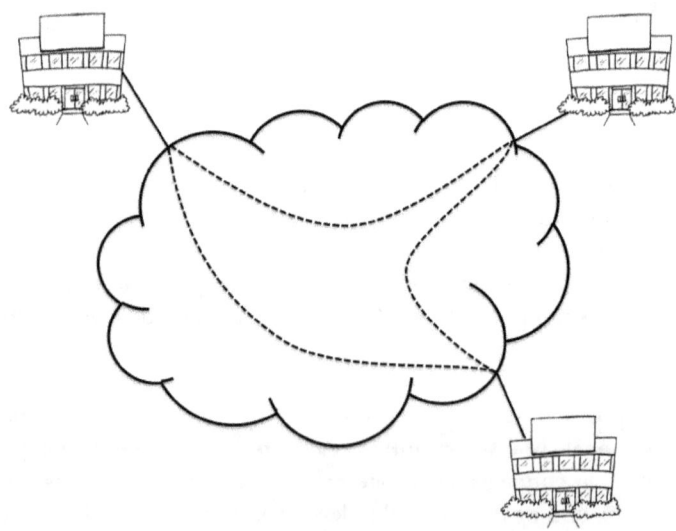

The Network Cloud solution is much more cost effective when building networks and takes advantage of various economies of scale when it comes to the cables and the boxes on the end. So if one box can handle 100mbps of data, you could split it into 10 mbps 'virtual' circuits going to 10 different sites. The second big benefit is when it comes to traffic flow. Many offices only work 9-5 so, after these hours, the part of the connection they are using may not need to be all 10mbs. You could therefore ask the network to, at 5pm, slow one connection down to 5mps and add that 5mps to one of the other connections that needs it, maybe a factory that takes data in to process production 24 hours a day. The combinations are really endless and this is where the art of the technical sales consultant comes in with the salesperson, helping the customer work out the best and most cost effective way to use the service.

Pros of Ethernet Services. *Seamless.* Two LAN's can look like one, creating a 'seamless' network for the customer. They don't need to know or care that a WAN is involved.

Economical. When travelling short distances, it can be a very economical service to provide, given that everything needed is supplied in the solution.

Responsiveness. Computers and the applications running on them will operate in exactly the same way and speed regardless of which location you are in.

Secure. As this is a 'discrete' service, in that you don't share cables with other companies, you have the same security as traditional point-to-point services.

Cons of Ethernet Services. *All Traffic Is The Same.* Ethernets do not prioritise traffic. If you are trying to play video or voice across a LAN, the network doesn't know that it is voice traffic and treats it the same as any other. Therefore, you may be in the middle of a video call but if the network is flooded with traffic, the picture could degrade or stutter.

Control Of The Box. Given that the box, which connects the customer to the service, is provided by the supplier, it is often the case that the supplier has total control over that box. This may be an issue for some companies as they maybe concerned with security or control over their local network, which is the traditional demarcation point between the internal IT teams and the suppler teams.

Key Sales Messages

- Secure
- Direct
- Simple
- Cost Effective

IT departments do not need to worry about the complexities of WAN services.

All sites appear seamlessly to each other.

Equipment doesn't need specific configuration to work with a WAN as they will see it all as a LAN.

Solution Sales Message

The client doesn't have a knowledgeable in-house networking team and the cost of getting one would be prohibitive to them.

They are not a technology-focused company and want things to be as simple as possible for them.

Flexibility is key to their thinking and they want to be able to grow their services over time.

IP VPNs

Point to point services are good but have issues in economies of scale and price. Ethernet services are easier but have limitations on control of traffic. IP VPN's address these problems and also add a layer of functionality above and beyond that of those services. But it can also be a much more complex solution to deal with. Let's first look at some basics the sales person needs to know.

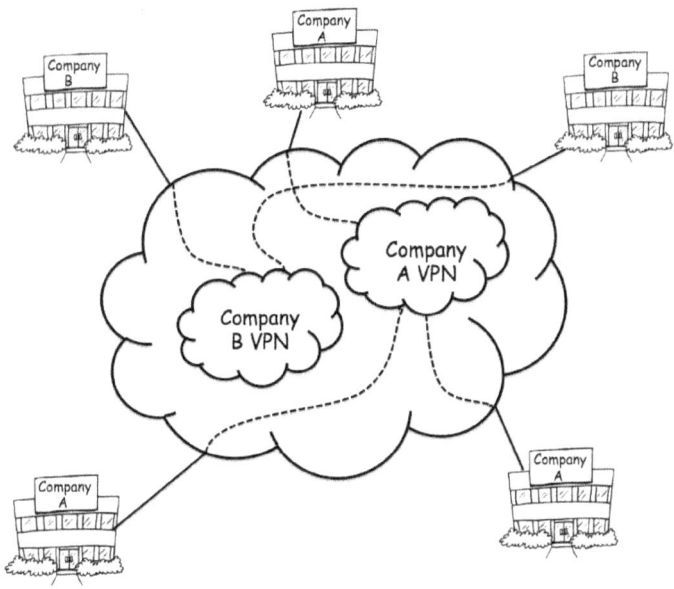

The IP part of IP VPN stands for Internet Protocol. This is the language that computer systems natively speak (we mentioned Ethernet earlier, IP is a layer on top of the Ethernet standard). IP has become ubiquitous in the world, mostly because it is the core language the Internet uses to communicate. Introduced in 1974 by Vint Cerf, it is essentially an 'addressing' system which allows little bits of information to travel around any network and contains the information needed to get from where it starts to where it needs to go. The closest analogy to IP is the postal code/zip code system. When you send a letter, the postal sorting office that picks up the letter from the post box looks at the first few characters of the post/zip code. This tells them the general area the letter needs to be in and sends it there. Once it gets to the general area, the post sorting office there looks at the last characters of code to find out exactly what delivery round that letter needs to go out on. The delivery person then looks at the building number and street name to deliver it to the exact address. IP works in the same way, except each packet (letter in our analogy) has both the IP address (the post/zip code) of where it originated and where it is to be delivered. It makes for a very efficient delivery system that is scalable to millions of devices all around the world.

The VPN part stands for Virtual Private Network. Point to point and Ethernet services are inherently private networks as you get dedicated use of a connection from point A to point B. A VPN on the other hand is private in a VIRTUAL way as, although your data will flow across cables with other people's data, the system inherently keeps each packet of information private and has security in place to make sure a packet can only be read by the intended recipient company.

There are two types of IP VPN, those that use the public Internet and those that use private networks (that is, private to the supplier, such as BT or AT&T). For those that use the public Internet to make VPN's, all the hard work is done by the computers at each end of the connection. The computer wraps the package of data up in a wrapper that can only be opened by the computer or system at the other end that is allowed to open it. Although the packet will then travel along the public Internet, it is securely wrapped enough so that VPN's are inherently secure, so much so that companies and governments all use VPN's and trust the data that goes across them.

However, to be even more secure, companies can access private VPN networks. By private, I mean networks that are owned by a supplier and they control who can and can't access them. They also allow the network to do other, more complex things that the public Internet is not set up to do. The main technology to do this is called MPLS, or Multi Protocol Label Switching. Multi Protocol because, even though it uses the language or 'protocol' IP in most cases, it doesn't have to, it can use other protocols. Label Switching because the packet is 'switched' or routed from point to point on the network depending on the rules on the 'label' attached to that packet. And the rules are one of the extremely powerful things about these networks.

Regardless of the information sent from your computer to another, or your device to another, the device splits the information into little chunks (packets) before it sends them out. Now, although they may leave in the correct order, things often happen in a network that the packets reach their destination in a different order. When it comes to an email, this is not a problem as a computer is clever enough to reorder them before it shows you the email on the screen. However, if someone is listening to an MP3 music file for example, if the song is split into little packets and gets to you in the wrong order, you won't really like the resulting sound! It would be all jumbled up and sound horrible. It is even worse if you are trying to have a voice conversation with someone else via your PC or an IP Telephone. If the packets of information (as in, your voice) do not get there both in the right order and in the right time, it's not going to make for an enjoyable conversation.

The big benefit in this network is that you are allowed to put rules in place that makes some traffic travel faster or get priority over others. So, if your packet is going through a network and it is your voice, the network will move other packets that are not so important out of the way so that yours gets to their destination on time and in the correct order.

The use of IP VPN's has grown exponentially over the last decade due to their flexibility and the levels of control you have over how the network works. From a practical point of view, when a customer wants to build an IP VPN (on a private network), each site gets a point-to-point connection between it and the access pop (point of presence) of the suppler (by pop, we mean the providers actual physical location of their network equipment). As the connection enters the supplier's premises, it connects to a box that has a unique id. This box then connects to every other box in that supplier's location, and that supplier's location is connected to each of their other location. The supplying company then places rules on that box that tell it which other box id's it is allowed to talk to. So, if you connect from one office to pop A of your supplier, and your second office connects to pop B of your supplier, the box at pop A may be given the id 'A123', and the box at pop B may be given the id 'B456'. When any data enters box A123 from your first site, a rule is placed on it that says 'this data can only be seen and come out of the network at box B456. This means that data from many companies whom the supplier provides service to can travel on the same network, but can only be seen by the various end boxes that have been given permission to see them.

If you then want to add a third site to the network, you simply install a point to point line from your new site to its closest pop, connect it to a box with a new id (say 'C789'), and then update the rules to allow A123, B456 and C789 all to see each other.

An Internet based IP VPN works in the same way. The originating device 'locks' the information in a packet and tells it what its destination is and has a 'key' that allows it to enter the end destination. The key it carries allows it to enter the device at its destination, and this device holds the key to then unlock the packet. The only real difference between the public and private networks is that, in a private network, the flow of traffic is controlled, where as in the public network, traffic is in a free for all and has to fight its way to its end destination and has no priority over the other traffic also trying to get to their destinations.

Pros of IPVPNs. *Flexibility.* Regardless of what you want to do with the network, be it just data, data and voice or data, voice and video, you can set the network up however you wish

Future Proof. IP is very much the standard in the world and all systems are designed around IP as a communication language. Also, as the system is rules based, if there is a change in how the company works, the customer can reconfigure the network accordingly

Cons of IPVPNs. *Complexity.* Deciding on the rules of the network can be complex and needs to be thought out by the customer to get the most effective use of the network.

Price. To make full use of the network, each site needs enough bandwidth to be able to use all the types of data it wishes. Although cheaper connectivity methods are available (such as broadband lines), broadband is not a technology that lends itself to this type of network. Ideally, each site should have its own dedicated circuit.

Key Sales Messages

- Flexible
- Scalable
- Multi-Use
- Future Proof

Run voice, video and data all over the same network.

No single point of failure in the network.

Future proof technology that can be reconfigured as needed for the business as things change.

Solution Sales Messages

Your client speaks of flexibility and efficiency in how they want to run as a company.

Adopting new ways of working, such as using video communications and Voice over IP (VoIP) services to enable their staff to work better is of interest to them.

They are open to making a 'step change' in how they work as an organization and are looking at their communications as part of an enabler for the company.

Internet Connectivity

At a basic level, Internet connectivity is simply a connection between you and your Internet Service Provider (ISP). You have a connection, be it fixed or wireless, from your location to the location of your ISP. Once your connection is made, the ISP then sends your data across its own network until the point it connects to the network where your information is destined to go. The Internet is therefore 'a network of networks'. Each ISP connects to each other ISP (either directly or via other ISPs) to allow them to swap data between them. How fast and effectively you can communicate across the Internet depends on the speed of your connection to your ISP and also the speed of the connection at the other end of the destination you are trying to reach. So, you could have a fast 50 mbps service, but if you are trying to get information from a computer in another country that only has a 1mbps connection, the fastest you will get that data is at 1mbps.

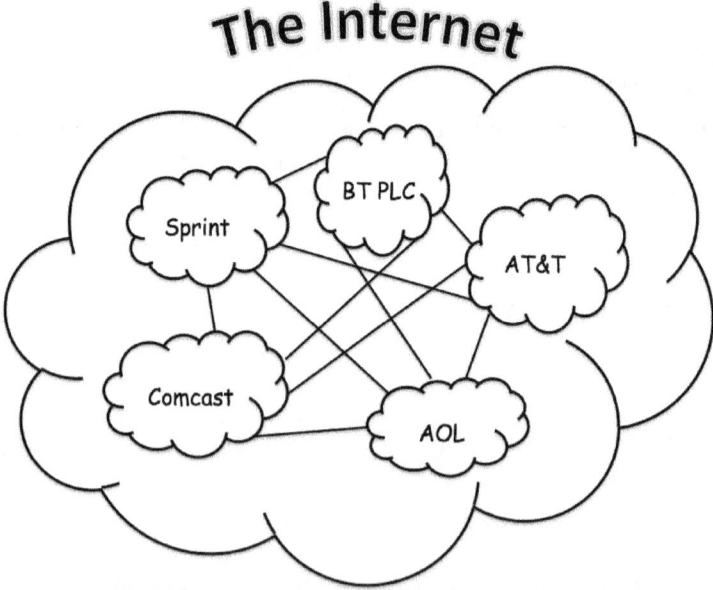

When it comes to Internet connectivity on a company wide basis, there is a trade off between cost and usage. Say you have an office with 1000

members of staff, each of whom want the internet to be as fast as they get it at home, say 5mbps. If all the staff uses the connection at exactly the same time to its full capacity, they would expect to need a 5000mbps (5gbps) Internet connection (1000 x 5mbps). This would not be a very cost effective way to run a network. Realistically, most people don't use the full capacity at any one time, and not concurrently. Also, not all staff may be in at the same time and the vast majority will only need it between 9-5, Monday to Friday. When you take all these factors into account, a 1000 person site could comfortably work with an internet connection of 50mbps or less and still have a better experience than their home service.

One of the major differences between home Internet connections and office Internet connections is how the actual connection to the Internet is made. Virtually all home Internet connections use a service called Broadband (ADSL, SDSL, CABLE). Broadband is a way to have many people connected via a single Internet connection, much the same way as in an office. However, unlike an office, you are not sharing with people you know, but with anyone else in your local area. Although many offices also use broadband for their connectivity, they will tend to pay for premium services that give them a better connection (less contention or sharing) than the public broadband service.

If your company relies on its Internet connection to work, it is more likely that they have a connection based upon a point-to-point service. This gives them a dedicated and guaranteed speed for their users to connect to the Internet and means they are not affected by other companies using the service. However, they will still only go as fast as the connection of the destination computer they are trying to communicate with.

Internet connectivity is becoming an essential for organisations to do business. Both their suppliers and customers expect to be able to communicate with them via the Internet and email services in this day and age and companies that do not embrace this are falling behind. This has meant a change in the way Internet connectivity is seen and relied upon by its users. In fact, some countries are so concerned about this, given that many government services for the public are only available on line, that they are looking at internet connectivity becoming a 'right' of people to have access to, in the same way as water and power are.

There are also many things a supplier can do to enhance the service they offer their client to stop Internet connectivity being a commodity that goes to the cheapest provider.

Managed Services. As the internet is a open network, there are many people out there trying to do things that are illegal or immoral, from trying to break into computer systems, becoming infected by viruses and to looking at inappropriate pornographic images. Many suppliers offer to protect you and manage your service so that you don't have to worry that your company is exposed to these issues.

Variable connections. As mentioned, an average office only needs their Internet connection from 9am to 5pm, Monday to Friday. Why should you therefore pay for a service that is available 24/7? Suppliers offer many customers reduced rates that give them a high speed during core working hours, but then slow the connection down outside of the working day. The supplier can then take advantage of this by offering other companies whom maybe work different hours access to use the speed they have freed up.

Email services. Probably the core reason companies use the Internet is to enable their employees to send emails. So important is this that many suppliers offer to manage this all on behalf of their clients. This frees up the internal IT departments to work on software and systems specific for the company and not have to worry about this day-to-day task.

Pros of Internet Connectivity. *Ubiquity.* The vast majority of businesses today have an Internet connection and can therefore communicate directly with each other, electronically.

Accessibility. A companies customers can get to them and their services or information about the products they provide. In fact, many people now do all their purchasing online and therefore will only deal with companies who have a presence on the Internet.

Information. One of the biggest benefits of the Internet is the volume of information available. This means that staff can get access to information the company needs in an easy and cost effective way

Cons of Internet Connectivity. *Security.* By connecting to the Internet, you effectively open a gateway to your company that people could attack. The need for security at this point of the company network is key.

Time Effects. Giving your staff access to the Internet is a great enabler. But it is also a potential time waster. People are very conversant with the Internet today and use it for many personal reasons including shopping, banking and keeping in contact with friends. By having access to this resource at work, they could potentially be doing their personal things during working hours.

Key Sales Messages

- Ubiquity
- World Wide ecommerce
- Essential
- Speed

Communication with customers and suppliers is key.

Access to the vast amount of information available will enable staff to work more effectively.

The public expects to be able to communicate and find information about the company, 24 hours a day.

Solution Sales Messages

The Internet is the way the client does business but are concerned about security.

There has been a recent high profile 'hacking' case in the news and the client is aware of it and wants to discuss how it may affect them.

Live, online, real-time collaboration could aid the company in how they do business.

Data Centres and Hosting

So far, we have concentrated on the connectivity solutions that make up the core of data network services. However, over time, these services have become more and more commoditized and companies have been looking for other services associated with data networks they can offer which enhance their offerings to clients. One of the first natural steps was to offer what are known as data centre and hosting services.

In the general company environment, there consist two different types of system or device, that of the personal system (desktop, laptop, tablet, mobile device) and that of the server system (those devices that are accessed by multiple people), such as payroll systems, databases, websites and the like. If an individuals computer system fails, then it would tend to only affect that person. If a server system fails or people have a problem accessing it quickly, it can affect the whole company. These servers therefore need to be taken care of, stored in the correct environment and kept running at optimal speeds and connections. This involves having dedicated places to store these devices that have controlled power and temperature so as to ensure they are available at all times. They also rely on complex backup solutions, from making sure there are multiple copies of the data to having duplicate hardware available should they develop a hardware fault that needs replacing or fixing.

Although companies can do this themselves, there is an economy of scale available to companies who can provide this solution to multiple companies in controlled environments; with vast air conditioning systems and resilient power delivered from multiple parts of the electricity network.

Although some use the terms data centre and hosting interchangeably, there is a distinct difference between the two.

Hosting: Hosting services refer to situations where a company's data and systems are stored and run on equipment owned by the supplier.

Data Centre services: This more correctly refers to the situation where a companies own equipment (such as their computer servers) are placed into the controlled environment of their supplier, where the supplier ensures the power, security and temperature requirements are maintained, but the equipment is still owned and managed by the company

You will often hear other terms such as co-location (which refers to a companies network and telecoms equipment being stored in someone else's location) or Virtual Hosting (where you are given a part of a server as opposed to a whole physical server). However, from a business perspective, these services are all about letting someone else provide the physical storage and location services of your equipment so as you don't have to be concerned with the intricacies of power and temperature management within your own office space.

Telecoms companies are extremely well placed to offer these services as, over time and through the build out of their own networks, they usually have a vast infrastructure of buildings that they own and have been specifically built to store and power electrical equipment. In fact, in many places, telecoms companies are the biggest property owners in the whole country. They have not always been the quickest to capitalize on this though and the new generation of service providers in the data market often take the investment of building data centres upfront in their business decision processes and therefore, although they may not have as many locations as the telecoms companies, those that they do have are located so as to make as best use of their services as possible.

What do we mean by best use? Well, some of the factors a company will be concerned about in regards to these services are things like distance (is the data centre physically close to them), resilience (is there more than one data centre and are they suitably far away from each other that something which impacts one would not impact the other), and accessibility, as in, if they need to send one of their own engineers there, how easy is it to get to and access.

Pros of Data Centres and Hosting. *Infrastructure.* The customer does not have to worry about providing controlled space for equipment and the intricacies of doing this.

Physical Security. Data centres are 24/7 facilities with round the clock security. If the customer's normal offices are only open during working hours, they will save on the cost of needing 24-hour security at their site.

Dedicated Infrastructure. Data centre facilities will be built around having the necessary core network infrastructure to ensure the optimal level of connectivity for server systems

Cons of Data Centres and Hosting. *Location.* As the equipment is not on the customer's own site, they may need to send staff there to maintain and repair the equipment if any issues arise.

Cost. Depending on the clients needs, if they are normally happy with a server sitting under someone's desk in an office and the risks associated with that, moving to an environment they pay for may be prohibitive for them. However, if they understand the need for dedicated environment services, this should not be an issue

Key Sales Messages

- Cost Effective
- Capex to Opex
- Resilient
- Continuity

Dedicated secure environments, monitored to ensure optimal conditions for equipment.

Business continuity is key to the organization.

Reduction in IT risk.

Solution Sales Messages

The customer wants to focus on their core business and not the business of looking after equipment.

They have experienced downtime from power failure within their own offices.

IT risk is something they need to minimize in their business or the client talks of having small, lean IT teams within the organisation.

Cloud Services

Probably the biggest buzzword of the 2010's is the word 'Cloud'. Traditionally used when talking about networks, the more modern use of the word cloud is in conjunction with the word 'Services' and refers to the movement of process that traditionally have occurred locally on a users computer or a companies servers, now taking place inside the computer networks of suppliers. This outsourcing of systems and processes makes sense for lots of reasons, not only cost. The primary of these is the changing dynamics of the workforce, needing access to information regardless of where in the world they are, what time it is and, more importantly, what device they are using to access it.

To explain further, let's look at a practical example, the use of CRM (Customer Relationship Management) systems. CRM systems enable all parts of a company to record and maintain information about their customers to better serve them. Traditional CRM systems have been developed in companies, for use on specific systems and have been notoriously inflexible. But the power and usefulness of CRM systems have meant that the workforce needs them to be more flexible than any other internal system in regards to customer service.

Salesforce is a cloud based CRM system launched in 1999 by Marc Benioff, Parker Harris, Dave Moellenhoff, and Frank Dominguez. The primary aim of Salesforce is to enable 'anywhere, anytime' access to a company's customer data, via any device that can access the Internet. This 'internet access' methodology is key to cloud services as Internet access is the ubiquitous communications medium of the world and is agnostic of the device that is accessing the data.

Following on from the success of such systems, many other companies in the software market are moving to delivering their solutions 'via the cloud'. One of the latest and most noticeable entrants is Microsoft and its Office software suite. Microsoft Office has been the standard in word processing, spreadsheet and presentation software for over a decade but, up until recently, accessing these software packages has meant installing a large package of software locally on a computer or device. This ties the user to a specific computer system to produce their office documents and is inherently inflexible. Google addressed this when it introduced its 'Google Docs' service. In Google Docs, the software to produce and edit documents was stored inside the network (in 'the cloud') and was accessed via the Internet and a web browser. However, the industry standard has been Microsoft and, with its latest incarnation of Microsoft Office (2013), their business model for these products has firmly moved to the cloud. When you buy Microsoft Office today, you have various options open to you. You can still buy the software on a disk to install on one computer. However, the preferred model from Microsoft is for you to 'rent' the software on a monthly basis and then have access to it both on your own computer and also via any computer with an Internet connection.

There are two aspects to this model, firstly the move by the supplier (Microsoft in this case) from a capital purchase model (where you pay once for the software outright) to an operating purchase model (where you pay monthly as an operating cost for your business). This generates a more robust revenue stream for Microsoft and a recurring income. Secondly, this move from Capex to Opex (Capital expenditure to Operating expenditure) is extremely beneficial for the client, as it does not rely on a large upfront outlay of cash they would have when purchasing the software outright. Over time, the client will probably end up spending more money overall but, as we will see in the chapter on selling to the CFO, the availability of cash can outweigh the negatives of a higher lifetime cost of the software.

Other benefits of cloud based solutions are that, as the processing takes place in the cloud, the need for powerful computing at the user level is less, meaning that cheaper, lower cost devices can be provided to the work force. Additionally, as the software is stored 'in the cloud' and you only access it when needed, you can be sure the software is always up to date as it is maintained by the provider, and does not need the user to load additional components to their local machine.

The over riding plus of cloud solutions however are their flexibility, both for the end user, who gets to access the software they need at any time, but also for the client companies, with smaller companies getting access to 'big company' solutions, and big companies getting granular management of their end user licensing and access to the solution.

Pros of Cloud Services. *Accessibility.* Cloud services offer true anytime, anywhere solutions to a company and its staff. It provides a level of flexibility for people to work, regardless of location.

Cost Reduction. Cloud services, when provided by others, can drastically reduce server hardware and maintenance costs for a company.

'Utility' Based Billing. Many cloud services are billed by the amount you use. This gives the company an excellent way to control costs and only pay for what they need at any one time.

Cons of Cloud Services. *Security responsibility.* All of the security of data is in the hands of the supplier. This can be an issue, especially in regards to sensitive data.

Dependency. A company can become extremely dependent on a cloud-computing supplier over a very short period of time. Should the supplier in some way change the service so it is not conducive to how the company needs to work, they could suffer issues.

Key Sales Messages

- Scalable
- Flexible
- Opex to Capex
- Availability

Anytime, anywhere access to your companies systems.

Cost savings on hardware and infrastructure.

Standardisation of IT requirements and licensing.

Solution Sales Messages

You client talks of having a flexible workforce, needing to be able to work from anywhere, at any time.

Capital expenditure is difficult from them at this moment so moving to an operating expenditure base would be advantageous.

The client will be either up scaling or downsizing in the near future and would like a service that can grow or shrink with their needs.

Virtualisation

The average user takes advantage of a very small percentage of the power of their computer most of the time. In addition, the average company uses much more computing power during their core hours (say 8am to 6pm) than they do at the rest of the time. When a company buys a server (a big, multiuser computer) for a certain system they are running (maybe their payroll system), that server is, most of the time, only using a small percentage of its available power. However, at the end of the month, when all of the pay slips for the companies' employees need to be calculated, the server is struggling to cope with the demand placed on it. This is a perfect scenario for virtualization.

Put in its most simple form, virtualization is the ability to take lots of physical hardware and, within the software of that hardware, build multiple 'virtual' servers that look, to the end users, like real servers sitting in the network. However, these 'virtual' servers have the ability to grow and shrink in size depending on the demand placed on them. So, for the first 25 days of the month, the payroll system only needs 5 'cores' (think of each core as a computer brain) to cope with the work it needs to do. But, for the last 6 days of the month, the payroll system needs 15 cores (15 computer brains) to cope with the work asked of it. In the virtual environment, you could then simply allocate more cores to it during those times and, during the rest of the month, let those cores go and work elsewhere.

Although an extremely simplistic view, that is the central method by which virtualization works. You install hardware that, in total, has an ability of X computing power. That X level of power can then be split up into chunks to be used by various parts of the company, as and when needed. This is as opposed to the traditional way where each system is given its own hardware and whatever power that hardware has, that is what it gets to use regardless of if it needs it or not.

In this respect, virtualization is like an extremely effective, multi capable task force, adapting to the needs of the company along the way, focusing on one system or process when needed and, when that process requires less work, shifting the resource to another process that needs it.

Like many other solutions we are discussing, there are possibilities for vast economies of scale. A good example of this was the recent Olympics in London. A one off event, many companies found their need for computing power was, for a few short weeks, much higher than ever before. They could have bought lots of new equipment to cope with this but, as the demand increase was only for a short period of time, this would have been a wasteful exercise. Those companies which ran a virtualized solution would simply be able to 'increase' their needs for that few week period and, once the Olympic fervour died down, could simply revert back to their pre-existing level of power.

One of the first companies to take advantage of this type of services was Amazon, with its Amazon Web Services (AWS) platform. Amazon had a vast infrastructure across the world to deliver its shopping services, 24 hours a day, 365 days a year to its clients. Because of this, they developed a robust infrastructure of datacentres at key points around the world. They realized the strength in this and started to offer these services out to others on a 'pay as you go' basis. Microsoft also offers these services in the guise of the Microsoft Azure platform, launched in 2010. Both of these are 'publically available', as in, anyone can purchase services in these platforms.

Many companies however do not trust these 'public' services and instead, either build their own environment (their own X amount of computing power to share between their companies departments) or take advantage of 'private' virtualization services where as supplier offers capacity within their virtualization setup but more strictly control access to it among its customers.

Pros of Virtualisation. *Flexibility.* The ability to both grown and shrink computing requirements depending on demands placed upon a company.

Asset Saving. By only using and paying for what is needed at any one time and reusing assets, virtualisation is an extremely cost effective way to run an infrastructure of servers.

Disaster Recovery. As the service is virtual, the ability to back up the structure and move it to new equipment is built in to most virtualisation offerings.

Cons of Virtualisation. *Complexity.* Managing a virtualised environment is a difficult skill, one that many IT departments will need to learn before they can move in this direction.

Vendor Support. Not all virtualisation services support all systems. Checks need to be made to ensure what a customer needs to run will be able to work on a particular solution.

Physical Failure. As one piece of hardware may support many virtual servers, if that fails, it will take down all of those services in one go.

Key Sales Messages

- Scalable
- Capital Reduction
- Efficient
- Performance

Cope with seasonal variation in requirements.

The ability to cope with changes in demand and the flexibility to both increase and decrease requirements.

Reduction in carbon footprint by only using what is required at any one time.

Solution Sales Messages

Your client is extremely IT literate and, as such, wants to be flexible in their services and respond quickly to demands.

Your customer has an expensive asset base of server equipment that would benefit from being rationalised and thus saving costs.

Your customer talks of issues around systems failing and the impact on the company when this has happened and could benefit from a more disaster resilient solution.

Unified Communications

For once, Wikipedia seems to have got it right and come up with one of the best definitions of Unified Communications I have come across.

'Unified communications (UC) is the integration of real-time communication services such as instant messaging (chat), presence information, telephony (including IP telephony), video conferencing, data sharing (including web connected electronic whiteboards aka IWB's or Interactive White Boards), call control and speech recognition with non-real-time communication services such as unified messaging (integrated voicemail, e-mail, SMS and fax). UC is not necessarily a single product, but a set of products that provides a consistent unified user interface and user experience across multiple devices and media types. There have been attempts at creating a single product solution however the most popular solution is dependent on multiple products.'

Let's break this down into its constituent parts and look at what is currently happening in the market. Instant messaging was the initial driver for UC once it infiltrated organisations and the benefits became apparent. Microsoft (MSN and Messenger), Yahoo and Google were the dominant companies who originally launched solutions (along with ISPs like AOL and CompuServe) that allowed you to talk live to other users through their services. You simply type you message, hit send, and it instantly appears on the screen of the recipient. Different to email in that this is a conversational system that relies on both people being on line at the same time. An extremely popular and cheap way to 'chat' with friends around the world, the business benefits were soon realised when you could talk to others across the company without the cost of phone calls and also with a 'different' method, (text as opposed to sound) that aided when sharing information.

But of course the need for both people to be on line at the same time meant that the solution needed to record your presence at the keyboard. It was a logical step to extend this into a person's presence in general, tying into calendars and other systems to say if the user was in the office, out on a meeting, busy or just not available. Once you link this with telephony, you get the ability for the systems to route calls and messages to people depending on this data. So, if your presence is set to 'in the office', any calls go to your desk phone. But when you are 'out', the calls are routed automatically to your mobile phone. Or maybe you are 'on leave' and therefore calls to you go to your voice mailbox or to another person in your absence.

Things take an even further step in combining all the various communications methods into one, with emails being read to you, voicemail being transcribed so you can view it in your inbox and all of them synchronised together, regardless of device or location. Add video into the equation as well and a true UC offering is an extremely powerful business tool. However, as the Wikipedia quote points out, although some companies have attempted to offer a single product (Cisco probably becoming one of the closest), UC solutions tend to be a mixture of different products from different suppliers all working together. Or so it should be because, as most UC users will attest, the fully integrated solution which works seamlessly is not the norm, suffering from the usual difficulties you experience when software and systems from diverse companies try to integrate between them, along with hardware from varying suppliers and devices from the likes of Apple, Microsoft, RIM and Google on the mobile side.

All of this shouldn't dissuade the sales person from this product set as, when it does work, it is an extremely powerful tool to put in the hands of the customer. Care just needs to be taken as there are bound to be issues regarding existing solutions integrating into the 'total plan', legacy services that don't play nicely with the newer systems, or simple incompatibilities from various suppliers who interpret the various standards in different ways.

If you do implement this, the control in the clients network is extremely powerful. To make UC work correctly, network monitoring is a key factor and this provides a wealth of data as how a company communicates in the data network world, giving the sales person a window on where there are bottlenecks or where a new solution or technology has become available that could provide cost and efficiency to the customer.

Pros of Unified Communications. *Collaboration.* Staff who can easily get in touch with each other and answer questions between them can be much more productive in their work.

Access. True UC keeps people in touch, regardless of where they are. This brings flexibility to the workforce and how they access communication to each other.

Cost Savings. By moving to a totally IP built communications infrastructure, a company can run everything on a single network, their data network, and remove their voice services network completely, relying on Voice over IP to take its place.

Cons of Unified Communications. *Interoperability.* Unless starting from a green field site (as in, a new location with no existing infrastructure), integrating existing services and systems can be complex and time consuming.

Vendor Reliance. Taking a UC offering from a single vendor generates reliability on that supplier. Should the customer wish to move away, it can be a timely and expensive move.

Key Sales Messages

- Enhanced collaboration
- Cost savings
- Single network
- Accessibility

Give a company's staff the ability to work and collaborate with colleagues around the company.

Ensure communications from outside are never sent down a 'black hole', being routed to a person regardless of how they make contact.

Bring efficiency to staff, allowing them to work and be effective, regardless of location.

Solution Sales Messages

Your client seems to have issues in regards to departments communicating effectively between them.

There are issues around customers not being able to get in touch with the right person or by customer communications not being answered in a timely manner.

You client needs to save costs in regards to inter office communication and running both a voice and a data network.

Part 3 – Selling

Basic Selling Skills

Before we get into the specific selling aspects that relate to data networks, let's begin with some basic selling skills that are applicable to all sales, regardless of the specialty you work in.

When working in a data network sales capacity, we are inherently 'solution salespeople', as in, we are solving a business need for our customer. We need to keep this in mind throughout all we do as, if we are selling a solution to a business need, we are much more likely to be seen as a partner in the customers eyes, as opposed to a supplier, and this generates a much more open relationship and one which can be cultivated long term.

Being a salesperson has its own set of skills. Some people find these skills easier to learn than others and some people seem to be born with them. However, everyone can learn to be a sales person, there is no 'black art' to selling as long as you stick to a few basic rules.

Rule number one: You must believe in what you are selling.

This is important for many reasons. If you believe in what you are selling, you will be happier in your working life. That happiness and enthusiasm for the product you are selling will spill over into you sales meetings and also make it easier to overcome objections as you will 'defend' your product through your own belief in it (in much the same way as being a fan of a football team, you're more likely to talk positively about them and find extolling their virtues much easier than you would a rival team).

Rule number two: Do not be negative, even about your competition.

Negativity in any way breeds negativity in your conversation. Although there is a need to ensure your customer questions the virtues of your company against another, this should be something that you lead the customer to through your companies/products positives, not your competitor's negatives. When people are in a negative frame of mind, they are much less likely to make a positive buying decision at that point.

Rule number three: People buy from people, so be a nice person.

This is one of the hard things to find a balance in when it comes to sales, as there can be a fine line between being 'nice' and being 'gushing' or overly 'smarmy'. You are the representation of your company/product in the sales cycle and, if you believe in your product (see rule number one), you are bringing something to the table so you do not need to 'suck up' to the potential client, just be a happy, positive, friendly person. Leave you own problems at the door, your customer doesn't care about them, not from a business perspective. Being a happy, positive person will make your customer want to see you, as opposed to tolerate seeing you.

These three rules are applicable no matter what your selling and are the prerequisite for being a successful sales person. Next come the techniques you can use to steer the conversations you are having with your customer towards a 'buying' situation. Although these techniques are very different, each of them leads your customer to a point at which they are open to a solution being provided by you and your company or product.

Technique one: SPIN

SPIN stands for Situation, Problem, Implication, Need. You can attend weeks of training to get SPIN selling down to a fine art. However, the basic premise is very easy to understand. It can work in various ways, either from a real 'situation' or from an imagined one, although working from a real situation not only makes the whole thing more real for the customer but also shows that you are thinking about them and their problems. Let's look at SPIN in action in a real case in regards to a data network sale.

You attend a meeting with your customer and they mention that they are waiting for some documents to come in the post before they can get on with a piece of work. The SITUATION is therefore that the customer needs something to get to them before they can do their bit within their company. They have to have these documents sent by post as they include photos and computer aided design documents that are too big to put in an email and they are also concerned as to the security of the documents in transit. The PROBLEM is therefore that your customer is often sitting around wasting time while waiting for the arrival of documents, which means the delivery time to *their* customer is longer than it should be. The IMPLICATION is that they are potentially losing customers to competitors who can provide a shorter lead-time on their products. There is therefore a NEED for a way to get these documents safely and securely sent to his department in a much quicker way.

You are now at a point you can look in your 'kitbag' of solutions and offer your customer something that will address his need.

SPIN can be incredibly powerful as it makes you listen to your customer, the biggest skill you need to be successful in sales, and therefore look at addressing your sale to them and their need as opposed to some 'selling point' you have been provided by your marketing department.

Technique two: FUD

Fear, Uncertainty, Doubt (FUD) is a something that can be used to make you customer question their own processes, systems and organisation. Although fear is a negative emotion (something we don't want to dwell on), it can be a useful opener to get your customer thinking about what they need to make their company run better. The fear element is not something that should come directly from you (as in, you shouldn't say 'aren't you scared that xxx is going to happen') but is something that the customers should ask themselves following on from your questioning techniques. So, a good opening question in a FUD scenario would be 'How does your company run its back up policy?'. Your customer will tell you about what they do to make sure company data is resilient and, during this, with more open questioning, you can lead the customer to look at possible weak areas in their back up policy. This generates the FUD feelings within them that, if you have picked up on, you can positively respond to with a solution which will remove those fears, uncertainties and doubts from their mind.

Telling isn't selling

How long do you think someone can concentrate on what you are telling them? It depends of course on how interesting the subject is but, in general, if it's not something they can immediately see the benefit of or have a prior interest in, it's about 30 seconds. This is why product led sales presentations rarely work. If you're talking about some fancy new network system, only those who are already interested in network systems will be able to maintain attention on what you're saying. This is especially prevalent in 'C' level contacts as, due to their extremely busy schedules, they do not tend to concentrate on the details of things, leaving that to others who work for them. Telling people something isn't a good sales technique. Discussion on the other hand brings people into the conversation and makes it relevant for them.

American President, Harry S Truman, famously said;

'The best way to get your children to take your advice, is to find out what they want, then advise them to do it'

There are many correlations between how to work with children and how to work with senior executives, mostly because of their attention span, which is necessarily limited by time. No one, especially people who run companies and have a level of autonomy, want to be told what to do. However, engaging in a discussion and leading them to the solution to their problem in such a way that they come up with it is much more conducive to your relationship with them.

Pick the subjects you want to get to in your conversations and lead them there through questions. If you watch political debates on TV, you see that the person who asks the question leads the way the discussion goes. When chatting with your customer, the task is to get to their thoughts and feelings on the subjects you need to discuss to get to the solutions you want to provide.

Use listening to think

When asking questions, there are two great things about keeping quiet and listening. Firstly, you get much more information from the customer if you just listen. The second, and often more important, is that you get time to think. This helps to steer communication in the direction you want to by picking points from the customer's answers that you can use to lead in the direction you want.

Persistence is key

In your sales discussions, persistence can be key to finding out information. A direct answer to a direct question can be hard to come by, especially if you are dealing with a 'seasoned' procurement person who is guarded in how they interact with their suppliers. But, as the saying goes, there is more than one way to skin a cat. Asking questions in different ways, maybe by breaking it down into sub questions, is one approach. For example, a customer might not tell you directly about how much bandwidth they need at each site, but by asking how many sites and how many people, you could do a comparison to any other customers of similar size and what their requirements were. But don't also be afraid of being persistent for a direct answer. Just ensure you explain why you need the answer and what it will allow you to do in providing them a better solution to their needs.

Solution selling

Once you have identified a need your customer has through one of the techniques mentioned, you are well on the way to your sale. But do not make the mistake of jumping in with 'right, have I got a product for you that will solve that'. Selling is often described as a dance and a dance only works when both partners are moving at the same pace, understanding each other and their signals. You should use what you have discovered to show your customer you understand them and their needs in running their business. The first point in solution sales should be just that, replaying what you have heard back to your customer, either verbally, in a document or in a presentation. You should also ensure that, at the end of this replay process, you get confirmation from your customer that you have understood them correctly. There is nothing more irritating to a customer than you going into a sales spiel about your fantastic product that will address their need, only to have misunderstood the need in the first place!

Now you have your customer's agreement and you are all coming at a 'solution' from the same viewpoint, you can then begin to outline what would be required to successfully address that need. We have not talked about 'products' at all so far and still won't. Remember, a customer wants to know what difference something will make to his company, not that he will have some super new technology. So, in our SPIN example from the previous chapter, we would at this point be talking about how a faster process will generate better customer satisfaction for their clients and make them less likely to go to the competition. This is the point at which your customer gets into a 'buying' mind set as you are talking about something that will help move their company forward.

We can now look at the solution from a product sense. But be careful here in that we should only be talking about the product in a way as to how it addresses their requirements (such as security, speed etc.). You can also include the other, great aspects of your product, but only if you can relate that aspect back to a benefit for the customer. Again, throughout this, ensure you get your customers agreement that the aspects you are 'solving' are correct for them and their business.

Now we have identified a customer need, empathized with them as to that need and what will be the benefits for them of addressing it. We have then looked at how that need would be solved and what you can offer them to solve it. We're now at the part of the process that many salespeople struggle with, closing.

Closing is the term for getting that all-elusive signature on the contract. This is where all your hard work has lead. But it's not as simple as just finishing your presentation and then pulling the contract out of your bag. This is where the dance really begins and you get into rounds of negotiation and specification. These aspects usually happen with less senior members of your customers team as they are the 'details' which the CEO does not have the time to get into. But before getting into this potential minefield, it is important to get a positive buying commitment from the customer who has the final say. One approach is to get verbal agreement that, 'if we can work out the details on this, is it a solution you would feel is worthwhile for your company'. If you have done all your homework correctly, the answer should be yes. This therefore leads you to the actual sale where you create a tacit agreement between you as the sales person and the client who has the final say that, should everything else be ok once you have gone through the 'details' (and make no mistake, price is just a detail), they would take your solution forward. This gives you the license to spend your precious time outside the meeting negotiating internally to get the discount you need to make the sale happen, to ensure that your company is also positive about this sale and that the promises you are making to your client will come true.

That tacit agreement is important, as it is your ticket to you next meeting. This leads you to your final question, 'What date can we meet again to finalize this?'. This gives you a time frame both internally and with the customer's team members as to when you need to have a fully costed and approved solution ready for the signature of the senior person. This next date should be a celebration of your two companies working together and the actual signature becomes a formality.

There are many other aspects to solution sales than this short chapter can address. If you want more information as to sales in general, feel free to contact me via my website, ask questions of others on the site, or look for sales training courses both within your organisation and externally.

Selling is like playing golf. It takes five minutes to learn but a life time to master.

Research

Regardless of if it's a new client whom your company has never done business with, or a company with whom your company has a long history that you personally are taking on as a client, the relationship starts with your research. Obtaining as much background information as you can about your prospective client is the foundation stone of your relationship and the one aspect that salespeople I have worked with seem to be least likely to do (usually giving lack of time as the reason why). My answer to this would be 'would you go for a job interview with a company having not researched them?'. During most professional interviews, you are asked what you know about the company, its history, what it does, its values, and if you fail to answer, it can be the death knell of your job offer. Talking to a prospective client is analogous to a job interview. You're effectively being interviewed as someone they will potentially be working with for months or years to come, just like a new employee. The difference is that they won't be paying you a salary for a service, but they will be paying your company large sums of money for a service that you will be instrumental in delivering for their company.

Having explained the importance of research, the question is WHAT to research? Since the Internet, research has become much easier and really breaks down into a few specific areas.

1. The view they want the public to have of them.

Every company wants to project a certain public image, be it to their customers, their shareholders, their potential investors or the public at large. The easiest way to see this is from their own website and marketing materials as these will have been carefully crafted to ensure they reflect the view they want the world to have of them.

2. The raw data on the company.

Looking at the share price history of the company (I find Yahoo! Finance to be one of the best places to do this) will give you a good understanding of the ups and downs of the company over the past years. You can also see any major shareholders who have bought or sold shares in the past year and have to declare them publicly (such as the CEO). This is good insight into the health of the company, if those involved are buying or selling their shares at any one time. If you can, it is also worth getting the annual report of the company. This will give you an idea of where they have invested their money in the recent years, if they have made any large capital purchases and lots of other useful information. They may seem daunting at first and understanding even the basic financial statements in them can be an 'art' in and of its self. There are many resources available on the Internet to help you understand this information, including using the blog and discussions on www.deanwevans.com where you can ask for help from me or other users of the site.

3. What the news says.

A general search for the company you're interested in will show not only their site but also mentions of them on other sites. It's good to focus on reports or information from news outlets applicable to your customers market segment. So, for example, in the IT and Telecoms arena in the UK, an excellent news source is The Register (http://www.theregister.co.uk). Having been around for a number of years, The Register provides both generic 'tech' information and news, but also allows you to drill down into specific areas, such as Networks, Mobile, Hardware and the like. http://info.retail-week.com is a similar news site focused on the retail sector, and http://www.pharmiweb.com focuses on the pharmaceutical industry and what is happening in that industry.

4. The key people.

The professional version of Facebook is LinkedIn. LinkedIn allows people to put their professional CV/Resume online and then connect to others whom they do business or work with. It also allows you to show info publically and you can find out a wealth of information about individuals from this site. Although not everyone uses this, many more are joining on an on going basis and, over time, it's becoming the de-facto standard across the industry.

Not an exhaustive list but by using these 4 areas and taking information from each, you will be able to create a picture of the company and its key personnel. Once you have this information, you need to distil it down to the basic facts and what actually matters. A good rule of thumb is that all of this together should not cover more than 1 A4 page. If it does, there is probably more information there that you need to know or can cope with.

HOT SALES TIP: Type 'case study (customer name)' into Google. It's a great way to find out if anyone has undertaken a substantial piece of work on your customer as, if they have, they are likely to have published a case study about it as a way of advertising their services. Case studies will not only tell you what was done for your customer, but often will also tell you when a contract was signed and how long it was for.

Making Connections

One thing that many sales people struggle with is getting connections with 'C' level clients. Most sales people will be pushed by their company to get connections at this level, as these people are the decision makers within a company. However, to get to this level, unless you have other contacts you can use to get you there, it can be a long process, working your way up through the various lower departments until you make your high level contact. There are some strategies you can use to help you get there;

1. Ask for introductions. You will tend to have most success this way as people do have a tendency to trust recommendations from others. The adage 'it's not what you know, it's who you know' is true in the sales environment. You should preferably use business connections to make these introductions but, if need be, you can use personal connections but make sure you are 'ethical' in doing this and not causing possible problems for your personal friend, using such an introduction for business purposes.

2. Use your own 'peer' level contacts. If you know a CTO in one company and they think highly of you and your services, ask them to make introductions to their peers across the industry. People in specific job roles are often involved in exhibitions and conferences and make a wide circle of colleagues across other companies and, as long as you are in good standing with them, are usually happy to provide an introduction.

3. Sell up the ladder. Try to get to the highest ranking person you can but keep an eye on their hierarchy and look to get introductions to their manager, even just initially getting to say hello to them or inviting them out for lunch or some other event.

4. Also use these lower level contacts to find out the needs of the business and then come up with proposals that you can ask to take to higher individuals in the organisation. The only thing

you need to be careful of is that people lower down the structure tend to focus on how things are done, more than what needs to be done. You'll need to be able to read between the lines to turn a 'how' into a business 'what'.

5. Use your own suppliers to see whom they talk to in the industry and get connections that way. As an example, if you sell a particular package of equipment from your supplier for one of your customers, ask them who else buys that package of products from them and can you make a connection.

6. Also look for connections you have in your customers suppliers who can make that all important connection for you. As long as the product they are supplying is not in competition with your own, they will usually be willing to do this.

7. Look for companies whose products compliment those you sell and see if you have a route to a contact there. This is mutually beneficial for both organizations and something you can build on long term.

Once you have gone through these routes and have exhausted them, there is always the ability to go back to the personal letter approach. But I do mean personal. In this world of email and electronic connections, a personal letter to an individual can get attention where electronic mail doesn't. The success of this approach will depend a lot on your letter writing ability and there are many books out there that will guide you on this, but the key thing needs to be that it is personal to the individual and also to the company and what you have found out about their needs. Anything within it that makes it seem like a generic marketing letter will result in it swiftly ending up in the bin! Also, make sure you print and hand sign the letter as well, which adds immensely to the personal nature of this communication.

'C' Level Selling

Selling to the CEO

At the top of the tree, and the target you are always pushed to get to, is the Chief Executive Officer (the CEO). The CEO has the ultimate responsibility for the company and therefore the ultimate responsibility when it comes to the purchases they make, especially the high ticket ones. Making a sale at the CEO level will give you almost carte blanche to work within the organisation and sell your products, as long as you keep cultivating this relationship.

The mind of the CEO is constantly being challenged with a thousand and one issues, even though they only really care about the big, strategic things, they still have to know about and are inundated with small issues. It makes conversations with the CEO exceptionally hard as you need the level of your communication to be at the 'Big Picture' point, but also being aware of what that will mean down at the lower level. What the CEO needs from you is to believe and trust that you understand their business and will therefore only take up their time with conversations that are important. Many a relationship has been soured when an Sales Manager wants to get in front of a CEO to talk about a new product they are pushing, when the Account Salesperson KNOWS that the solution is not one that will excite the CEO.

This is one of the fundamental differences with selling at the C level as opposed to lower down the tree. Business managers within a company are focused on the immediate needs today for the company, be it cost savings, enhancements or other things that directly impact today. CEOs are interested in this AND things which will impact the company long term, be it a change of working practice or mentality, or a development which will build over time to affect company culture. This makes it a rich vein in the world of big solutions, such as cloud services and unified communications especially.

More than any other individual in the organisation, the relationship with the CEO is more important than any other aspect. Although they care about the details of the sale and what you are providing, what they really care about is the benefit it will give the company and *how* you give it is a secondary consideration. That means that, as long as you have a good relationship and you deliver, any issues that may arise, unless they are substantial, are less of an impact than with others within the organisation.

When it comes to cultivating this relationship, status is important. More than ever, you need to mimic their language and style back to them. If they are someone who talks in broad-brush strokes, you need to talk in broad-brush strokes too to guide them to the conversation you want to get to. If on the other hand they are more detail orientated, then you must also be detail orientated.

Action is the byword of CEO relationships as their time is extremely precious. The most important actions are those you can get allocated for the CEO themselves, but this is extremely difficult. If you can get the CEO to commit to an action to do something, then you are in an extremely powerful position. But, at the very least, the one committed action you need at any CEO meeting is an agreement on a subsequent meeting. As said at the beginning of this chapter, cultivating the CEO relationship is extremely important, very hard to do and very easy to lose.

Even without actions from the CEO, YOU need to commit to actions yourself (with the agreement that you will get to report back on them to the CEO at a later date). Actions are the way a CEO copes with the plethora of information they have to deal with. The volume of meetings they have means that they rely on notes and minutes from meeting as an aide memoir when they next have to deal with that person or issue again. I once heard one CEO of a very large multinational corporation say 'if there's no action point against it, it didn't happen or it's not important'.

Although not exclusive to CEO communication, you need to keep in mind a few of the communications basics about relationship building. The first of these is the personal relationship building aspect, the small talk. CEOs, even though their time is more precious than any other contact, still need to feel comfortable with you as an individual. You need to keep small talk brief but you do need it to be there. A point from the news which has a very tentative link to them or their company is a good subject area at first, but family and children are always a point once you develop your relationship as they are the universal leveller of most people in their lives.

The next big point is strategy. As stated, CEOs have a 'bi-focal' nature, in that they are both worried about that month's performance, and also about where the company will be in 5 or 10 years time. If you can engage this level of conversation, around the strategy of getting there, you will be able to identify opportunities along the way. A tip though is not to jump on one strategic point immediately but absorb it, think it over, and bring it back in another meeting, showing that you are thinking about their company, even when you are not there with them.

Attention getting is a key in turning from discussing to selling. In all solution sales, we are selling on the benefit. The CEO things in the big picture so you need to get their attention with simple big solutions, things that will have enough impact on their company that it is worth the CEO's time to work with you and not palm you off on another person lower down the hierarchy.

Finally, paint a picture of what their company will be like with your solution in place, which marries their own vision of the future, and places your company at the heart of achieving the goals of the CEO. The more vivid and detailed picture you can paint, the more it will stick in their mind and become part of the picture they will paint of the company's future.

Selling to the CFO

The Chief Financial Officer (CFO) of an organisation is the person who holds the purse strings. In their own way, they are a more important decision maker than the CEO. This is mainly due to how they have obtained that position in their career. Usually accountants by training, their understanding of the companies finances are relied heavily upon by the CEO and the board of directors as it is a skill set they may not have. The CFO understands the balance between the companies' debts and credits which, from the view of people who have an interest in the company (i.e. the shareholders and investors), is the most important thing.

Because of this outlook, the CFO has different triggers when it comes to what they are interested in when it comes to the products the company buy. But do not make the mistake in thinking that price and financials are the ONLY interest they have. Again, like the CEO, they probably have a personal investment in the company and, unlike an external shareholder or investor, the CFO is much closer and more aware of how the company runs and what impacts its growth or decline.

As a stakeholder, getting the agreement of the CFO has two stages. Like the CEO, the first agreement has to be that the solution you are selling has a positive impact on the company, either solving a problem or enhancing them in some way. The second agreement is in regards to the commercial aspect, one of which being the price but, more over, the terms of how that price is paid. Let's look at an example of how price in a financial deal comes second to the term.

When working in banking sales, I used to always hear the following little 'aide memoir' when it comes to what is important to a CFO.

'turnover is vanity,

profit is sanity,

but cash is king!'

Let's look at this in more depth. The turnover of a company is, in its simplest form, how much money flows THROUGH a company. If you wanted to run a $1,000,000 company, it's easy. You just need to buy something from a supplier for $1,000,000 and then sell it to a customer for $1,000,000. Your turnover is now a $1,000,000. But your profit is $0! The reason why it's termed a vanity is that companies like to quote turnover as, even in small companies, the turnover figure can be huge and, although we shouldn't be, everyone is impressed by a large financial number.

But as mentioned, the profit is $0, which is where the 2nd line comes in, 'profit is sanity'. A company who buys their supplies for $999 and then sells them for $1000 is less successful that one that buys its supplies at $8 and sells them at $10, as their profit margin, the difference between the buy price and the sell price is greater. This is without taking into account the 'cost of sale', that is, how much it costs you to run your company to then sell your product (office space, staff, packaging costs, storage, etc.). A companies profits say how successful they really are in actually making money. If a company can prove that it makes a profit year on year, making more money than it costs to run, by a large enough percentage, then that company is more successful, more people will be interested in its shares and the higher value we place on that company. The quintessential example of this type of company is Apple Inc.

So why is profit not king? The problem with profit is that it is a value based over a period of time. Let's say you run a small company that can buy 100 widgets at $10 each. However, to get those 100 widgets, your supplier needs you to pay for them in advance and they take 30 days to deliver. So you need $1000 for 30 days. You have a customer that is willing to pay you $20 a widget for them once you have them, but as they are bigger than you and have a strong position in the market, their payment terms are 30 days AFTER delivery. So now you need $1000 for 60 days. You have an extremely profitable business but if you don't have the cash which you can tie up for 60 days, you cant make your business work.

'Cash is king' is really the key to running a growing business and something the CFO will have foremost in their mind. Having cash in the bank, money they can get hold of as soon as they need it, is extremely powerful. It puts the company in a position to react to changes in the market as and when they need. So, for example, if their factory uses a lot of oil to run, and they expect the price of oil to double in the next 3 months, if they have cash, they could buy lots of oil in advance at todays price and mitigate the problem of rising oil prices. Or, if they are negotiating with a smaller company who they know is 'cash poor' and need the money as soon as possible, they can make an offer to pay earlier for their product for a discount on the overall price. Cash is king as it gives you the ability to react and move much quicker than your competitors.

Keeping these rules in mind, you can see where a CFO is less likely to be stuck on the price of a solution than they would be on the cash flow of the business and how your solution will either 'open up' capital for the company or how they can save capital or mitigate the cost over the contract.

As a practical example, a solution which costs $50,000 is more attractive to a CFO if they can pay for it over the next two years than one which cost $40,000 but they have to pay it all in year one. If they can hold onto $25,000 for two years, it puts them in a stronger 'cash position' to be able to cope with any changes in the market.

Selling to the CIO/CTO

The CTO (Chief Technical Officer) or CIO (Chief Information Officer) of a company can be a difficult person in the solution sales arena. The reason being that they tend to fit into one of two categories. Technically astute, the CTO may be the type which is extremely proud and protective of what they currently have, usually when they are someone who has been with the company since its early days and they have 'grown up' with it, building the companies infrastructure as they went along. They are one of the few people who really 'know' how the company works from a technical perspective an it makes them an extremely valuable resource.

The other type is the 'professional CTO', someone who still understands the technical side but delegates the 'details' and is more focussed on the business benefits. Although all CTOs 'should' be like this, many are not or, those that are, are only interested in business benefits as they feel that they need to be to be on par with their other 'C' level colleagues where as, really, they are still very much technical people at heart.

Although these are very general statements, like most stereotypes, they are founded in reality. A lot depends on the type of company you are dealing with. A perfect example when it comes to the duality of 'C' level people would be a company like Facebook. Mark Zuckerburg, the CEO, started his life as an extremely gifted programmer. Although now, as a publicly traded company, he should be focussing on how the company works as a business, he also admits to working on the programming side still when he can as it is where he feels most at home. Although you would expect to sell a solution to him on the business benefits, if you cannot engage him in the technical arena, he is much less likely to be excited by your proposal.

When it comes to the CTO and selling data based solutions, you also have the other hurdle of their technical knowledge in competition to yours. There needs to be a fine line trod between you being able to talk about your solution, yet still making sure they are acknowledged as the 'expert' in the room as that is the view they will naturally have cultivated with their peers. If you come across in anyway as being more knowledgeable than the CTO on technical subjects, you may impress others in the room but may alienate the CTO. One of the easiest ways to cope with this is by directly referring to the CTO or 'checking' with the CTO, getting their agreement that you have done something correctly when explaining a technical issue.

Things can be different in a one to one meeting as they are more likely to WANT your knowledge, so as to increase their own. At that point, you can cultivate an extremely positive relationship with the CTO as their 'trusted advisor'. The best way I know to do this is to find out something they are interested in which is technical but not connected directly to their business (so that it doesn't become contentious in any way). A good example would be if you notice they seem to always have the latest gadget or phone. If, in the more personal moments of a meeting, you mention some new piece of news you have heard about the latest mobile phone, you will likely engage them in conversation and position yourself as their peer in regards to a shared area of interest.

Many sales people are wary of CTOs and their technical knowledge. However, this is not needed as, given that you are a sales person selling technical based solutions, your own knowledge is higher than you might give yourself credit for and being less of an expert than the CTO is never usually a bad thing, as long as you are knowledgeable 'enough'. And given you are working through this book, you will be!

CTOs are bombarded by sales people trying to sell products. Now, unlike others at the 'C' level, they may actually like to hear about new products and services as they have the responsibility for choosing the best IT for their company and therefore, on an on-going basis, they need to pay attention to the new technology appearing on the market.

So what does get them interested? Usually one of the following will get them to see you; Product, Price or Relationship. Product, if it is different from what the competition offer or a new technology you have an edge in. Price, if you are drastically different (as in, lower) than the competition. Relationship, if they already know and trust you. But most CTOs will not make an initial purchase based on relationship. Partly because CTOs tend to be more 'tool' orientated than their peers, but also because they are so very busy that relationship building is low on their list of priorities.

High on the list of things on their mind is fear. Like a soccer goalkeeper, their job has a leaning towards stopping bad things happening more than making good things happen (a goalkeepers role is to stop the ball going in your teams net and not to score in the other teams net). Bad things for a CTO include lose of data, systems failing, or a competitor achieving an advantage through a new technology they themselves haven't adopted. But one of the other big fears for a CTO is that they will run out of time. They usually work in fixed periods of projects or role outs and they can be in constant fear that they will run out of time or that projects will deliver later than that which they told their peers they would. This could lead to them having a negative profile with their peers at the board level in regards to what they are tasked to achieve, which could lead to them moving on.

Your job is to therefore eliminate as much fear and risk from their lives as is in your power. The risks can be financial in nature as IT departments are a cost to a company and rarely an income, and therefore work to tight budgets. Technical risk, such as security and resilience issues is another, and change risk, where technology is constantly changing over time and the company needs to keep up with the competition and marketplace. But one of the biggest risks to address is job risk for the CTO, going back to the soccer goalkeeper analogy again. The CTO rarely is involved in things that make a profit for the company directly and therefore are not the 'star' of the company, but can easily be seen as a failure if they 'let in a goal' if there are security issues or if sites and systems fail.

All of these lead us to some general things we can do in a CTO relationship to position our companies and ourselves in a positive light.

1. Provide reference material about similar companies in the customers sector who use your solutions. This not only helps mitigate risks for your customer in their decision making (if XYZ ltd trusts you, then you're ok), it can also prompt further discussions about the varying approaches that different companies take to achieve their desired result.

2. Get the CTO to sign a non-disclosure agreement (NDA) with you and then share some new or upcoming technology your company is working on. This builds a level of trust and the ability for the CTO to feel 'ahead of the competition' as they

are aware of things that their competition may not know about.

3. Look for financial proposals that provide a net positive impact for them. Budgets are finite and IT is a cost to a business so if you can provide a solution that either reduces cost or provides an income stream, this is extremely positive. If this is not possible, work on long term deals which have less impact either at the beginning or the end of the contract term, depending on what is important to their company's current financial position.

Selling to the IT Department

Unlike a CTO/CIO, the IT department is more interested in the day-to-day impact of any possible solution. As the individuals whom need to work with the solution and become the conduit between it and the end users, they can be one of the hardest groups to 'sell' to. The status quo is often the remit of the IT department as they are aware of their workload and are wary of a new solution that may have an impact on that. Surprisingly, that concern over the impact is both if the solution saves them time as well as if it increases their time. With more and more IT solutions being outsourced, an internal IT department will be very negative with any solution that takes them and their skillset out of the equation or negates the need for them in the organisation.

The IT department can also have an effect on decision making greater than they should. This is because of the lack of understanding by senior teams as to technical issues, which makes it easy for internal IT individuals to steer a board in which ever direction they wish, playing down possible benefits and highlighting and enhancing possible negatives to the solution you are looking to provide. Careful consideration must be taken when it comes to this aspect of the sales process and getting the 'buy in' from these teams.

However, it is not all negative. An IT team and its individuals are, by their nature, interested in technology and this is a scenario where you can really call on your technical colleagues across your organisation to help in the sales process. As internal technical teams do not often get involved in company wide events, in the same way sales teams do in 'kick off' events and the like, attention that you put onto the IT team, inviting them to events, giving them demonstrations and such, letting them contribute and play with the solution, pays more dividends for you than in many other departments.

Any solution you provide must tick the technical boxes of the IT department. They are, in the car buying analogy, the one's who will be interested in the 0-60 time, the engine capacity and the top speed. This is the one area you can focus on the product specs that are often so highly valued by your own internal product departments. You will of course have to defend your product against those of your competitors, especially where a competing product may have better specifications than the product you are offering. Use your technical colleagues to do this but with one caution. My experience has been not to involve those colleagues that are the actual product owners within your company. The reason behind this being that some aspects of a product can be subjective as to those that are better or worse than others and someone who's job it is to produce products for your company can be extremely defensive about the choices they have made in developing something. Therefore, take disagreement from the technical people in your customers organisation in good cheer, explaining why your company took the approach it did, without stating that the other approach is wrong in any way, just different.

Hands on demonstrations can be quite key in driving this point home. The more you show your product to the technical members of your client company, getting them involved in testing, even giving them equipment on loan to 'play with', the more you will build your relationship with them. Inherently distrustful of sale people, allow IT departments hands on time with a solution, showing you have nothing to hide, will help gain their buy in on any solution you propose.

Sales Hints and Tips

Finally, I want to share with you a few hints and tips you can use TODAY to improve your sales success. They are in no particular order, just little nuggets of information I have personally come across and used over my sales career that have proved themselves time and time again.

1. Before going into a customer meeting, look at their share price over the past 12 months (if they are a publicly traded company). This gives you a lot of information. Firstly, is the company on the up or on their way down? This will have an impact on their buying ability at any level. If a company is experiencing a downturn in shares of 12 months or more, you can almost guarantee that they will have internal barriers to spend in place. It's a typical knee jerk reaction by company boards in this situation. Secondly, it gives you an opening question for the customer to talk about as, especially at the senior level. Many employees are also shareholders and the share price is something they will be aware of and will also have thought about how to make it better (maybe with help from their 'partner', such as your company?)

2. Listen to radio shows or podcasts (my favourite) about your market sector and find at least one 'nugget' of information in regards to something that is happening. It not only gives you a subject area to discuss but, 9 times out of 10, you will be giving your customer a piece of information they don't have. This positions you as a source of information for them, something people in business find valuable and ups your profile.

3. When it comes to point 2 (or any other 'news' item in your customers sector), have an opinion! Holding a fluid conversation on a subject shows your interest in it. Just mentioning a subject and not having a view can lead you down the path of stumbling for a conversation, where as having an

opinion (even if it is different from your customers) will open up the lines of communication.

4. When you go into a client's reception and sign in, look at whom else has signed in too. I've found this a great way to find out if your competitors have visited your client as, when a client is in the market for something, they will often put aside a day or half day when they take meetings from the various suppliers.

5. KEEP YOUR MOUTH SHUT! For new sales people and old hands alike, you can get much more information by not saying anything than by saying something. But be aware, this only works when your customer is talking about a subject they are passionate about (either positively or negatively). If you try this when they are talking about something they don't care about, you will just get an uncomfortable silence,

6. Match your customer's attire. Too many companies feel sales people have to be in suits and shiny shoes, where as research has shown that, when building a sales relationship, it's much more important to be on par with your client. Men, if they don't wear a tie, take yours off (before you go in). If they are in more causal clothes, you go in more casual clothes. But if they are always in a sharp suit, you make sure your dressed the same. This mimicry of the customers dress style generates an atmosphere of equals within the room, making them more comfortable.

7. Ask for your next meeting date at the BEGINNING of your meeting. This ensures you have a next meeting, even if this one is not as successful as you would hope. To do this effectively, open your notebook or whatever you use to write actions during your meeting as you sit down and suggest it's something you 'get out the way' before getting into the meeting proper.

8. Don't start your meeting with your company's life history except in one or two sentences. This meeting is not about the

key message of your company as it's not about you, it's about the customer.

9. Substantiate your claims and facts. Makes sure that any fact or figure you bring into the conversation you can back up if needed. It is even worth saying directly that you can show evidence if needed.

10. Try and make sure that you can equate benefits to any costs, preferably on a direct financial basis (as in, this solution gives you a return of X pounds this fiscal year), or in attacking a fear (this solution will ensure Y does not happen to your company).

Further Reading

Although this book tries to encompass as many ideas as possible, some subjects require much more reading than this book can contain. The following books are those that I can recommend and have helped me in my sales career.

Newton's Telecom Dictionary: Telecommunications, Networking, Information Technologies, The Internet, Wired, Wireless, Satellites and Fibre - Harry Newton

Publication Date: August 1, 2011 | ISBN-10: 0979387345 | ISBN-13: 978-0979387340 | Edition: 26th Edition

This is the world's bestselling and most comprehensive reference book on telecom, data communications, networking, computing and the Internet, with over 785,000 copies sold. Featuring 26,283 terms and hundreds updated and expanded, the 26th edition of Newton's Telecom Dictionary weighs in at over four times larger than any other telecom and IT dictionary, and includes wired, wireless, satellite, fibre and Internet terms.

It explains technical concepts in non-technical language anyone can understand. According to Discount Long Distance Digest, it "truly belongs on the bookshelf of everyone in the telecom industry. It's worth every penny, and is pound-for-pound the best telecom book we have seen."

The Ultimate Sales Letter: Attract New Customers. Boost your Sales. - Dan S. Kennedy

Publication Date: February 14, 2011 | Series: Ultimate Sales Letter Publisher: Adams Media; 4 edition | ISBN-10: 1440511411 | ISBN-13: 978-1440511417

In the age of e-mail and instant communication, great sales copy is indispensable to closing a deal. But too many sales letters end up in the junk file or the wastebasket. In this new edition of his top-selling book, author Dan Kennedy explains why some sales letters work and most don't. And he shows how to write copy that any business can use.

Understanding Company Financial Statements - R.H. Parker

Publication Date: 4 Oct 2007 | ISBN-10: 0141032715 | ISBN-13: 978-0141032719 | Edition: 6Rev Ed

The language of accounting and finance is presented in a clear and accessible manner. No previous knowledge of accountancy is assumed and the emphasis is on analysis and interpretation rather than accounting techniques. Referring throughout to the financial statements of actual companies, Professor Parker shows not only how to read a balance sheet but also what investors should look out for. He explains many important financial and accounting concepts, and deals with taxation, audit, profitability and return on investment, liquidity and cash flows, sources of funds and capital structure.

www.ingramcontent.com/pod-product-compliance
Lightning Source LLC
Chambersburg PA
CBHW072223170526
45158CB00002BA/717